MW01147959

TAR FOR MORTAR

Fig. 1. Hieronymus Bosch, *Ship of Fools* (1490–1500)

First published in 2018 by dead letter office, BABEL Working Group
an imprint of punctum books, Earth, Milky Way.
https://punctumbooks.com

The BABEL Working Group is a collective and desiring-assemblage of scholar–gypsies with no leaders or followers, no top and no bottom, and only a middle. BABEL roams and stalks the ruins of the post-historical university as a multiplicity, a pack, looking for other roaming packs with which to cohabit and build temporary shelters for intellectual vagabonds. We also take in strays.

ISBN-13: 978-1-947447-50-9 (print)
ISBN-13: 978-1-947447-51-6 (ePDF)

LCCN: 2018932399
Library of Congress Cataloging Data is available from the Library of Congress

Book design: Vincent W.J. van Gerven Oei

HIC SVNT MONSTRA

TAR
FOR
MORTAR

The Library of Babel
and the Dream of Totality

Jonathan Basile

For my parents. Without their support through my illness, this project would not have been possible.

they used brick for stone ... they used tar for mortar

Genesis 11:3

Contents

Acknowledgments

I would never have begun writing this book, or even dreamed of its possibility, had Eileen Joy not placed a strange amount of faith in me by saying she would publish it. It owes its existence first of all to her, Vincent W.J. van Gerven Oei, and the creative risk taking of punctum books.

Its ideas have branched from too many diffuse roots for me to be able to trace them all or thank everyone by name. At the very least, I would like to thank Scott Goodman, Matt Howard, Rotem Linial, and everyone who joined the conversation at "Fictional Archives, Archival Fictions" at Good Work Gallery, Maia Murphy and everyone who made possible and took part in "Uninventional" at Recess Gallery, and the unique and fertile intellectual community of the BABEL Working Group.

Nor would it be possible to thank individually everyone who has shared a brief encounter and lingering insight with me through a visit to libraryofbabel.info. It has been the site of so many chance crossings, each of which has left its trace on the writing here.

Introduction

I came to realize, after facing several difficulties in the construction of libraryofbabel.info, that I was attempting to make a faithful recreation of an impossible dream. The website is an online version of Borges's "The Library of Babel," which I hope to show was imagined by its author as self-contradictory in every aspect, from its architecture to its pretense of housing all possible expression. I have not resolved these tensions, and so my project resembles Borges's library only by mirroring its failure. The Library of Babel was imagined as containing every possible permutation of a basic character set (22 letters, space, comma, and period) over 410 pages. This much is certainly possible computationally—the website now contains every possible page of 3200 characters from a similar set—but the dream of a universal library is still elusive. Beyond the contingent limits of its small set of Roman characters, the length of its books, and its medium, there are essential reasons why no amount of writing can exhaust the possibilities of meaning. A text exists in what Borges calls an infinite dialogue with its recipients, and its endless recontextualization guarantees that even without a mark of difference every book, page, and even letter can differ from themselves. Our libraries do not fall short of universality because of a character we've left out, but because totality itself is essentially incomplete.

In all its forms, the library should lead us to think differently about the possibility of originality or novelty. It was self-evident to the librarians in the Library of Babel that they could never create an original work; instead they hoped to discover the truth in the prefabricated texts they considered divine. But this feeling that possibility has been exhausted shouldn't depend on any actualization (such as printing out or publishing online an entire combinatoric set). Because language communicates itself as a structured set of differences, its basic units (in this case, letters and punctuation) will always be permutable. This permutability is universalizable: every form of expression and experience is dependent on signs or marks and a conceptual structure whose intelligibility precedes it. That is, even the most unpredicted or unpredictable event is intelligible to us only by means of conforming to pre-existing concepts and forms of experience. We are bricoleurs cobbling together and recombining found texts, without the possibility of immediate spontaneity. Even if our deployment of these signs is motivated by a momentary context, the library offers an overwhelming reminder of the indifference of all expression to these intentions. Borges himself played with the originality of his act of authorship, placing a disclaimer in the foreword to *El jardín de senderos que se bifurcan*: "Nor am I the first author of the tale 'The Library of Babel'; anyone curious as to its history and prehistory may consult certain pages of the magazine *Sur,* Number 59, which records names as diverse as Leucippus and Lasswitz, Lewis Carroll and Aristotle" (*Branching Paths* 5). Nonetheless, we will come to recognize just as much continuity as perfidy in his act of supposed non-authorship, which may be a universalizable condition of our relationship to history or tradition. There is no novelty, for the same reason that there can be no repetition.

A pure repetition, as Borges often pointed out, would disappear completely, lacking even a mark by which to distinguish it from its predecessors. We would not be able to recognize its existence or write these words contemplating it if there were no difference between our universal library and its predecessors. The lack of self-identity of our forms of expression guarantees that something resembling novelty will always take place, even if there is no mark by which to recognize it, and even if it is caused by nothing resembling our own agency or spontaneity. It may even be the very principle that undermines the sovereignty of the supposedly self-present subject. As a result of the deconstruction of invention and discovery, we will find something like repetition in every "new" experience, and something like novelty in every supposed repetition.

Borges treats the relentless emphasis on totality in "The Library of Babel," the narrator's claims that the library is infinite in space and time, that it contains not only every possible permutation of its character set but all possible meaning, with a gentle irony. Similarly, in his non-fiction he will assert at times that combinatorics could saturate literature or that repetition is the only reality, while at other times arguing that a single text differs from itself and that nothing ever purely repeats. Such irony and self-contradiction are the very forces that undermine the possibility of totalization. Their function in Borges's fiction and non-fiction will be the subjects of the first and second chapters (though we will quickly see that the distinction between fiction and non-fiction is difficult to maintain). The third chapter focuses on an ideologically motivated strain of literary criticism, which compares the internet to a universal library. These critics take for granted the completeness of Borges's Library of Babel; they both ignore his ironic undermining of totality, and exaggerate the power of our contemporary technology. Borges's writing pre-programs its technological progeny, not by containing a totality of all past and future possibility, but by playing with the gap that disrupts all identity.

The Library of Babel

The narrator of "The Library of Babel," a librarian living within its stacks, relentlessly asserts its totality and infinity. It contains all possible permutations of its character set, all possible meaning; it has existed always, will continue forever, and extends infinitely in space as well. Of course, none of these propositions could ever be verified by a creature conditioned by finitude, limited in space and time. Our narrator takes them on faith. There are several indications that Borges takes these claims ironically, not in order to denigrate the library (as though it could house all possible expression but falls short), but to show that totalizing expression is an impossible ideal. This irony mirrors a recurring gesture from his "non-fiction," where Borges frequently asserts a principle with a romantic or mystical appeal, one of unity or transcendence, while affirming elsewhere the premises of a deconstruction of that same assertion.

Despite the immense amount of literature about Borges, it is rare to find critics who question the veracity of his narrators. Much more frequently, the totalizing conceptions of his narrators are taken as expressions of Borges's own mystical inclinations. Whether among specialists, theorists who cite Borges as part of broader philosophical projects, or among more popular literature, one finds authors from Barrenechea to Foucault to Bloch committing this same oversight and incorporating into their texts the ideological illusions of Borges's narrator.[1] A more careful reading can identify an ironic narrative position in every story from *The Garden of Forking Paths*. The Borges who emerges from this web of textual self-contradictions is not the exuberant celebrant of mystical union but one who dances over the no less mysterious abyss that complicates the passage from finitude to infinity.

Architecture and Anarchitecture

The story opens with a vast vision of what may be an endless structure, a blueprint for an architecture that could, like the library's texts, iterate indefinitely, perhaps infinitely. This framework, of hexagonal rooms with four or five walls of bookshelves, with one or two passages to adjacent hexagons, with a vast pit either within or between them, is developed in one of the most textually complex sections of the story. Every one of the revisions and ambiguities of this paragraph, which seems to introduce us to the spatiality of the library, renders uncertain the form and consistency of its structure. Borges creates a text whose most intimate identity is a difference or conflict with itself — the readers who attempt with greatest dedication to be true to his design inevitably imagine structures that either contain gaps in themselves or create gaps in his story.

The textual uncertainties begin in the first sentence, which describes hexagonal galleries "*con vastos pozos de ventilación en el medio.*" The four English translators of this story are divided on how to interpret this phrase — either as "with vast airshafts

---

1   See, for example, Barrenechea's *Borges: the Labyrinth Maker,* Foucault's "Language to Infinity," or Bloch's *The Unimaginable Mathematics of Borges' Library of Babel.* From all the criticism I reviewed in the course of this study, the only explicit doubt of the narrator of "The Library of Babel" comes from Kane X. Faucher's "The Effect of the Atomist Clinamen in the Constitution of Borges's 'Library of Babel'" and Neil Badmington's "Babelation." The most insightful interpretation I have come across of ironic narrative position in Borges's stories, focusing on "Pierre Menard, Author of the Quixote" and "The Garden of Forking Paths," is Efraín Kristal's UCLA 118th Faculty Research Lecture.

between," according to James E. Irby, in other words, between some number of hexagonal galleries is an empty external space, or "each with a vast central ventilation shaft" (di Giovanni)[2] and "In the center of each gallery is a ventilation shaft" (Hurley). While there is no literal textual basis for the appearance of the word "each" in both of these translations, the phrase "*en el medio*" admits either interpretation. Though these three translators opt to disambiguate the opening sentence, the only one who maintains the uncertainty of Borges's phrase is Kerrigan: "hexagonal galleries, with enormous ventilation shafts in the middle." Here we see, in its very first sentence, an abyss opening on the infinite or what exceeds our capacities to the point of

---

2   Though Norman Thomas di Giovanni's translation of this story has never appeared in print, I consider it an important facet of the English-language reception of Borges. The majority of the English translations of Borges's work published in the author's lifetime were collaborations with di Giovanni. The pair worked together on much of Borges's poetry and his later prose works, but were unable to publish translations of some of his most important fiction, including stories from *El Aleph* and *Ficciones,* because the translation rights were still held by the publishers of an earlier English edition.

Borges's collaborations with di Giovanni are strange, loose translations that demonstrate more about the pair's theory of translation than they do about the original work. Borges was notorious, when translating other authors, for his creative infidelity, and was no more faithful to his own writing (on this theme, see Efraín Kristal's *Invisible Work: Borges and Translation*). Still, they clearly represented Borges's wishes, and it is unfortunate that after Borges's death, his widow and executor of his literary estate María Kodoma, in collaboration with Viking-Penguin, let the di Giovanni translations go out of print and commissioned the Hurley translations in order to circumvent di Giovanni's contracts (di Giovanni, "The Borges Papers"). Their likely goal was securing more profits for themselves from the English versions of the work by bypassing the 50/50 agreement Borges had made with his friend.

Di Giovanni has been barred from disseminating his (that is to say, also Borges's) translations, even being forced to remove them from his website. I stumbled across his otherwise unpublished translation of "The Library of Babel" on the internet's Wayback Machine; at the time of publication, it was accessible at https://web.archive.org/web/20130212202907/http://www. digiovanni.co.uk/borges/the-garden-of-branching-paths/the-library-of-babel.htm. I have salvaged whatever I could and made it available on my website, along with his out-of-print translations, at https://libraryofbabel. info/Borges/BorgesDiGiovanniTranslations.zip.

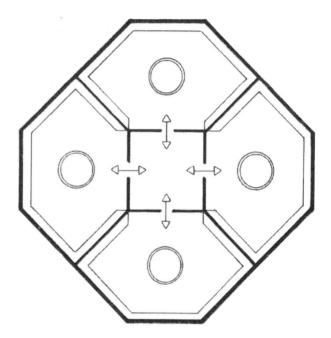

Fig. 1 — A node of the Library of Babel if only one of each hexagon's faces opened on an adjacent hexagon, as drawn by Cristina Grau in *Borges y La Arquitectura* (66).

suggesting infinity (the sublime), shifting across the border or shifting the border itself of the internal and external.

What follows is no easier to interpret or translate. The first edition of the story, published in *El jardín de senderos que se bifurcan* in 1941 or 1942,[3] read as follows: "*Veinticinco anaqueles, a cinco largos anaqueles por lado, cubren todos los lados menos uno* [...]. *La cara libre da a un angosto zaguán, que desemboca en otra galería, idéntica a la primera y a todas.*" Though there are other passages from Borges's 1956 revision that di Giovanni incorporates, here he relies on the first edition: "Twenty-five long shelves, five on each side, fill all the sides but one [...]. From the unshelved side, a narrow passageway leads off to another gallery, which is identical to the first and to all the others." Borges recognized an error in this text whose exact nature we will have to consider further, and made three changes, the substance of which was to free another of the hexagon's sides for passage to other galleries: "*Veinticinco*" became "*Veinte*," "*menos uno*" became "*menos dos*," and, somewhat strangely, "*la cara libre*" became "*Una de las caras libres*" — much of the controversy will rest on what became of this second shelfless wall. The other translators follow the revised edition, as Irby has it: "Twenty shelves, five long shelves per side, cover all the sides except two [...]. One of the free sides leads to a narrow hallway" (51). Resolving the uncertainties of this revision involves us necessarily in the physical uncertainty of the position of the ventilation pit, and the ontological uncertainty of the infinite and the finite.

Christina Grau, in her work *Borges y la Arquitectura,* explains the problem his revision was addressing and offers one possible interpretation of the envisioned structure (66). Though

---

3   The first printing of what is perhaps Borges's most influential collection is dated 1941 according to its colophon, but 1942 according to its copyright. The end of 1941 was the cut-off date for a national prize that Borges and his publisher hoped to win; the printing was either hurried to meet the deadline, or the date was falsified. Regardless, Borges's innovative work was passed over in favor of more recognizably Argentinian prose (see Jarkowski, "Cuando Borges Perdió Por Mayoría De Votos"). My thanks to Fernando Sdrigotti for his help in finding this explanation.

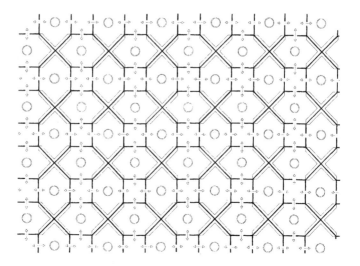

Fig. 2 — A floor-plan of the Library of Babel with two openings in each hexagon, as drawn by Cristina Grau in *Borges y La Arquitectura* (68).

the story frequently summons endless, labyrinthine expanses traveled by lonely librarians, a structure of hexagons with only a single opening would necessarily terminate at its first juncture (see Fig. 1). Such a structure is not capable of any expansion in the horizontal dimension, though it could repeat as endless, self-contained vertical shafts. If lateral movement were barred, it would be impossible to understand the first half of the narrator's melancholy recollections of traveling "for many nights through corridors and along polished stairways" (*Labyrinths* 54). Clearly, Borges meant to correct this design flaw when he revised his story in 1956. But the addition of a second passageway does not by any means resolve the textual problems in his opening paragraph. Grau still allows, in her diagram of the revised edition (68), for the problematic central square chamber (see Fig. 2). It seems, based on the circles in her diagram, that she opts for the interpretation that the air shafts will be inside each hexagon, and thus the central square chamber is an addition without a basis in Borges's text. Not only that, but "the idealists" among the librarians "argue that the hexagonal rooms are a necessary form of absolute space or, at least, of our intuition of space" (*Labyrinths* 52). While this seems to preclude the addition of a square room, it is at least not as explicitly forbidden as a room with one side more, or one fewer: "They reason that a triangular or pentagonal room is inconceivable" (52). If this square antechamber is meant to be the aforementioned narrow passage, we need to note that there are two for every hexagon and return to the third of Borges's revisions.

Antonio Toca Fernández, who responds to Grau's model in "La biblioteca de babel: Una modesta propuesta," suggests that Borges's revision is incomplete. Why remove the books from one wall of each hexagon, only to leave that wall closed off as a passage? He devises a minimal correction: what was *La cara libre* (the free side) in the first edition, and became *Una de las caras libres* (one of the free sides) in the second, should have been *Cada una de las caras libres* — each one of the free sides. This emendation justifies the dual openings in Grau's model, but her quadrilateral *zaguanes* still bother him. He recognizes that

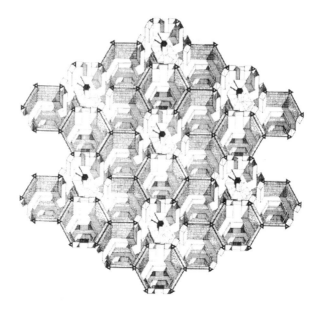

Fig. 3 — A floor-plan of the Library of Babel with two openings in each hexagon and a separate hexagon for each spiral staircase, as drawn by Antonio Toca Fernández in "La biblioteca de babel: una modesta propuesta" (79).

Borges wanted a structure that could saturate space with geo-metric uniformity and expands Grau's squares into hexagons (see Fig. 3). This model still contradicts several parts of Borges's text. The narrow passageways described by Borges open onto "another gallery, identical to the first and to all the rest." That is, they should provide communication between two hexagons, not six as in Fernandez' model, or four as in Grau's. And there's nothing narrow (*angosto*) about this passageway that seems to be swelling from one architect to the next, accreting new open-ings and disrupting the symmetry of the identical galleries.

A visitor to libraryofbabel.info, who identified himself as WillH, offered a clever solution that resolves some of these spa-tial and textual quandaries. It reinterprets the ventilation shaft "in the middle" of the hexagon(s), in order to evade the need to re-revise Borges's second edition. A single circular pit absorbs one wall of six hexagons, thus requiring only a single passage-way per hexagon, and remaining true to Borges's "*One* of the free sides" (See Fig. 4). His vision almost reconciles the textual conundrums, with one very significant *gap*. In an interview with Christina Grau in *Borges y la Arquitectura,* Borges explained his motivation for comprising his library of hexagons:

I thought in the beginning of a series of circles, because the circle produces the sensation of the lack of orientation [...] but the circles leave spaces between them that disturbed me. Later I decided on hexagons because they fit together with each other without needing other figures. (73, my transla-tion)

The elegant star created by WillH, though it is the only design that accepts all of Borges's emendations, and is the only one to read "*en el medio*" with Irby, leaves six spaces, each in the form of an empty or inaccessible hexagon, if we compress the pas-sageways or thicken the walls.

Should we accept only the evidence of the second edition, and claim that Borges's interview is extrinsic? But if he is being deceptive or dishonest, we should still reckon with his propen-

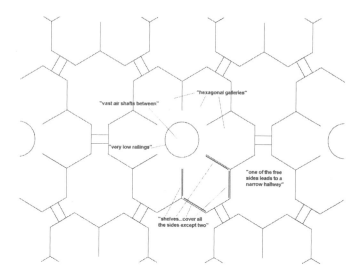

Fig. 4 — A floor-plan of the Library of Babel with one opening in each hexagon and the ventilation pit between a cluster of hexagons, as drawn by libraryofbabel.info user WillH.

sity for creating inextricable textual webs, labyrinths of revision and commentary that, like birdlime, trap the most careful readers the more we struggle for a coherent interpretation. I thought at one time that I could balance these tensions by accepting Fernandez's addition of a second passageway, and condensing the passageways into thicker walls (see Fig. 5).[4]

But I no longer long for a solution — I'd much rather marvel at a text that manages, seemingly with as much intention as accident, to allow for so many elegant solutions while always leaving a remainder of irreconcilability. My ultimate disagreement would be with Fernandez's claim that:

> Borges' story is not a murky [*desdibujado* — sketchy, adumbrated] dream; on the contrary, his lucid nightmare describes the library with the precision of an expert… of an architect. […]. What surprises and disquiets with respect to Borges is that, in his blindness, he imagined a universe that could be built. (79, my translation)

It's rather the opposite — Borges has an imagination that surpasses lucidity to its dark hinter-side, the mind of what I would prefer to call an anarchitect, whose great vision was an ability to lead us into blindness. We will run up against this limit continually, for example, when we come to Borges's irony; the creation of a text in conflict with itself disrupts or deconstructs the task of criticism understood as the selection from among possible meanings, to open us to the possibility of the impossibility of meaning or decision.

---

4   Led astray by my desire to reconcile the text's difficulties, I altered the text according to Fernandez' emendation and unthinkingly ignored the demand that the hexagonal galleries be "identical." Varying the position of the entrance and exit passageways clearly violates this symmetry. This image was created by my sister, Sarah Basile, according to my specifications; I give her full credit for its elegance, and take full responsibility for its errors.

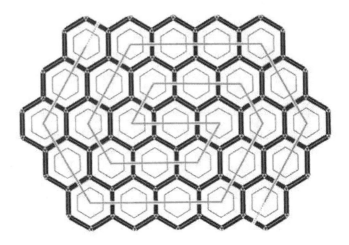

Fig. 5 — A floor-plan of the Library of Babel I imagined in a deluded attempt to reconcile the textual contradictions of Borges's revisions.

Dreams of Infinity

The story's opening paragraph, which grants entrance to this impossible architecture, closes by re-marking the impossibility of totality. After the repeating architecture is described, the story's librarian-narrator tells us:

> In the hallway there is a mirror which faithfully duplicates all appearances. Men usually infer from this mirror that the Library is not infinite (if it really were, why this illusory duplication?); I prefer to dream that its polished surfaces represent and promise the infinite…. (Borges, *Labyrinths* 51)

We just received a blueprint that demanded we be unfaithful either to Euclidean space or to the text itself, and that mentioned an abyssal pit shifting in and out of the center of the sanctuary. The mirror depicts another form of the infinite, capable of moving from the furthest reaches to the innermost heart of experience. The usual or vulgar interpretation of this entity is based on an infinity of extension, denied by the "men" who assume the mirror must be compensating for a lack in reality. The mirror image is more relevant to an infinity of intension; by allowing for an illusory, imaginary, false, or otherwise unreal gap, the mirror reveals the progression toward the infinitesimal that ceaselessly divides any hexagon, node, or point in this unstable field, and opens the lack of self-identity of any entity within the immediacy of experience.[5] Ironically though, the narrator shifts

---

5 Ana María Barrenechea's taxonomic approach to the Borgesian corpus appears problematic when viewed in this mirror. She attempts to create a stable set of categories or themes and to dissect Borges's works to fit individual scenes and symbols into her schema. With an analytic fervor reminiscent of John Wilkins's (see p. 63 below), she categorizes this mirror under The Infinite — The Infinite Multiplications — The facing mirrors, and places it among "the many symbols suggesting the infinity of the cosmos" that she claims to find in "The Library of Babel" (Barrenechea 39). Which cosmos, and which infinity? We have already found every word of this story to be doubled by the irony of a narrator with an impossible assurance about the endlessness of the cosmos, and by an infinity that slips effortlessly from the

this infinity off to distant, inaccessible reaches in an attempt to preserve his own dream of totality. Everywhere that infinity or saturation is invoked by the narrator, including the all-important claim of the combinatorial completeness of the library, he reveals only his vain struggle against the interdependence of structure and deconstruction, as well as the cunning irony of Borges.

The librarian decides dogmatically every one of the conflicts Kant attributes to an antinomy of pure reason. Kant uncovers the origin of certain traditional philosophical debates in a conflict of reason with itself, necessary to any finite rational intelligence. These antinomies include the finitude or infinity of space and time (quantity), whether there is a simple substance or whether matter is infinitesimally divisible (quality), whether there is intelligible causality, such as free will, or exclusively material causality (relation), and whether there is a necessary being or not (modality). Kant's argument is that none of these disputes can be decided either by logic or by experience, but that reason, as a faculty that seeks the grounds or principle of everything, necessarily uncovers these polemical pairs, without being able to resolve their opposition. Nevertheless, our narrator does what one should not, choosing the axiom that corresponds to his beliefs and groundlessly rejecting the other in each instance.

We are told repeatedly of the infinity of the library in both time and space. The narrator pretends to derive this idea from the purposiveness he sees in reality, though we know from Kant's *Critique of Judgment* the impossibility of determining whether such teleology is the work of natural or supernatural agency:

> First: The Library exists *ab aeterno*. This truth, whose immediate corollary is the future eternity of the world, cannot be placed in doubt by any reasonable mind [prime example of his dogmatism] [...] the universe, with its elegant endow-

---

outermost reaches to the inner heart of things. Eliding Borges's irony and ambiguity, as so many critics do, produces a one-sided reading of his unstable, undecidable texts.

ment of shelves, of enigmatical volumes, of inexhaustible stairways for the traveler and latrines for the seated librarian, can only be the work of a god. (*Labyrinths* 52)

We can clearly see here the arbitrariness of our narrator's reasoning. He thinks neither in terms of logic nor empiricism, but rather embraces any idea that celebrates the power of his preconceived notion of God (the necessary being). The attributes of his divinity are order, repetition, and the immaterial. We can see how this last attribute motivates his thinking in another of his reverent assumptions: "Once I am dead, there will be no lack of pious hands to throw me over the railing; my grave will be the fathomless air; my body will sink endlessly and decay and dissolve in the wind generated by the fall, which is infinite. I say that the Library is unending" (52). Though other traditions aver the finitude of space and time to make room for the divine beyond this realm, the infinity of the universe in all four dimensions is a way for our narrator of folding the immaterial into this world. His dream of infinite space allows him the possibility of transcending his body — not being left to rot within the confines of finitude and spatiality, but dissolving into an air that can almost be mistaken for the ether. The dream of bodilessness here also relates to a traditionally masculine fantasy of transcending gender, which we will return to when considering the all-male universe inhabited by the librarians. An explicit reference to Kant immediately follows this dogmatic assertion: "I say [*afirmo*] that the library is unending. The idealists argue that the hexagonal rooms are a necessary form of absolute space or, at least, of our intuition of space" (52). A classic dogmatic error is made in deriving the infinity of the universe from the necessity of space as a form of intuition — according to Kant, this guarantees only that a limit can never appear, and thus that empiricism is powerless to address the question.

The antinomy of quality stands out as the only one concerned with the infinitesimal dimension. These conflicting principles are no less necessary to the coherence of rational thought — the existence of a simple substance, one that would not be further divisible, is necessary to conceive of the stability or identity of any of the macroscopic structures composed of divisible elements. Nevertheless, infinitely divisible time and space are necessary forms of our intuition, so nothing indivisible could ever present itself to us. We will need to return, in the next chapter, to the atomist tradition that grappled with this question and which underlies much of Borges's story. For now, we can notice simply that the dream of totality, of a total library containing all possibilities of expression, is dependent on the existence of a basic set of atoms whose indivisibility is guaranteed. The second axiom set down by our narrator, "*The orthographical symbols are twenty-five in number*" (53) is a dogmatic assertion of the simplicity of the basic substance, element, or atom of this textual universe, which is the letter. The conclusion that their universal library exhausts expression is dependent on this assumption as well. The "thinker" who first surmised this thesis derived it from the existence of twenty-five symbols, and from a second premise, "*In the vast library there are no two identical books*" (54). This assertion is equally dogmatic, as it would be impossible for any finite creature to verify it. Furthermore, a fallacious logical deduction follows these unsound premises: "From these two incontrovertible premises he deduced that the Library is total and that its shelves register all the possible combinations of the twenty-odd [*veintitantos*] orthographical symbols" (54). Of course, the missing premise is the other equally foundationless assumption our narrator has accepted: the infinity of the universe. We can best understand the reason for Borges's ironic distance from an ideologically deluded narrator if we focus on what is perhaps the most fundamental of these misconceptions — that of the twenty-two letters.

There are reasons of both essence and accident for the insufficiency of the library's character set, all of which are re-marked by Borges. The accidental inadequacies are already enough to undermine the facile equation made between "all possible combinations of the twenty-odd orthographical symbols" and "all that it is given to express, in all languages" (54). Can twenty-two letters and three marks of punctuation express all the possibilities of all languages? If so, which ones? The number twenty-two must have suggested itself to Borges because of his interest in the Cabbalistic treatment of the twenty-two letters of the Hebrew alphabet. For example, in his essay "On the Cult of Books," Borges attributes the following sentence, which could be mistaken for an affirmation from our narrator, to the Cabbalistic creation story of the *Sepher Yetzirah*: "Twenty-two letters: God drew them, engraved them, combined them, weighed them, permutated them, and with them produced everything that is and everything that will be" (360–61).[6] A divine creation consisting of the permutation of twenty-two letters has an obvious resonance with our story; nevertheless, the alphabet used in the library is clearly Roman.[7]

Borges offers one account of a set of twenty-two letters capable of reproducing all possible text in his essay "The Total Library." Presumably starting from the 30-letter Spanish alphabet, Borges removes the duplicative double letters (*ch, ll, rr*) as well as the less unnecessary *ñ*. Removing *k* and *w*, letters appearing only in loan words, leaves us with twenty-four letters. Borges's account seems to pick up here: "The alphabet could relinquish the *q* (which is completely superfluous), the *x* (which is an abbreviation), and all capital letters" (215). In his introduction to *El jardín de senderos que se bifurcan,* Borges cited this essay as an account of the true authors of "The Library of Babel." Here he attributes both the idea and the dimensions of a twenty-two-letter essential character set to Lasswitz: "By means of similar simplifications, Lasswitz arrives at twenty-five symbols [*símbolos suficientes*] (twenty-two letters, the space, the period, the comma),

---

6 It is never a given in Borges's "non-fiction," but it does in fact appear that this citation is legitimate. See chapter 2, stanza 2 of the *Sefer Yetzirah* (100).

7 Kane X. Faucher, in "A Few Ruminations on Borges' Notions of Library and Metaphor," suggests that the library's character set must be the Hebrew alphabet. This assumption not only elides the questions raised by the implied transliteration of the manuscript of "The Library of Babel," but also ignores the complex textual history traced in "The Total Library" of authors attempting to reduce the Roman alphabet to these proportions — authors including Borges himself.

whose recombinations and repetitions encompass everything possible to express in all languages" (216).[8]

As is typical of Borges's writing, the textual web of this essay, his short story, and what we might incautiously call the true history is inextricably complex. At the very least, we can with some certainty refute John Sturrock, who assumes that Kurd Lasswitz must have been one of Borges's inventions, given that his name roughly translates to "weary wits" (100). He existed, was a German proto-science fiction author, and wrote "The Universal Library," a short story Borges rightly cites as an influence, though perhaps for the wrong reasons. The characters of Lasswitz's story share with Borges's narrator an interest in a subset of the library's contents: for example, the lost works of Tacitus or the true and false catalogues of the library. While Lasswitz's internal author says, "your readers will conclude that this is an excerpt from one of the superfluous volumes of the Universal Library" (243), Borges's narrator observes that "this wordy and useless epistle already exists in one of the […] innumerable hexagons" (*Labyrinths* 57). One thing Borges's library contains, though, that is definitely lacking from that of Lasswitz, is a 25-character orthographical system. Lasswitz allows for lower- and upper-case letters, ample punctuation and scientific notation, and ultimately settles on 100 symbols. Again, the temptation to tweak Borges's text ever so slightly presents itself, when we realize that Theodor Wolff, also mentioned in the essay, actually did propose reducing the character set to 25 in his 1929 *Der Wettlauf mit der Schildkröte*. After all, Borges first writes, "Lasswitz's basic idea is the same as Carroll's, but the elements of his game are the universal orthographic symbols, not the words of a language. The number of such elements […] is reduced and can be reduced even further" ("Total Library" 215), which seems to acknowledge that Lasswitz accounted for more symbols. Later

---

8   Both the "*símbolos suficientes*" and the wording and colon of the last phrase "*todo lo que es dable expresar: en todas las lenguas*" recall exact phrases from the "The Library of Babel." Interestingly, both phrases educe the aversion of translators, here and in most translations of the short story.

in the same paragraph, though, this is contradicted by the "Lass-witz arrives at twenty-five symbols" (215). Could he have meant to cite Wolff here? The situation is further complicated when we recognize that Wolff proposes a different 25 characters. Like Borges, he eliminates majuscules, numbers, and the despised q, but proposes restoring the classical union of i and j, replacing w with uu (corresponding to its name) or vv (corresponding to its shape), and declares z an abbreviation of sc or cs (Ley 246). No matter how we attempt to reconfigure Borges's text, we have to acknowledge some perfidy or betrayal in his attempts to disclaim authorship and give credit to his predecessors.

The situation becomes even more complex when we turn to the text of the short story. Before we reach its first sentence, the title confronts us with capital letters, and the epigraph not only contains numbers but speaks of another character set altogether. "By this art you may contemplate the variation of the 23 letters" refers to the classical Latin alphabet. The story goes on to use several of the excluded capital letters, digits, punctuation marks, and diacritics. A note from the "editor" offers little help:

> The original manuscript does not contain digits or capital let-ters. The punctuation has been limited to the comma and the period. These two signs, the space, and the twenty-two letters of the alphabet are the twenty-five symbols considered suf-ficient by this unknown author [*son los veinticinco símbolos suficientes que enumera el desconocido*]. (*Labyrinths* 53).

Uncertainties abound. Who is this editor? How are we to distinguish their interpolations from the original text? How should we attribute the other three footnotes, two of which appear in the first edition without reference to the editor, but indicated by the number one in parentheses, and the last of which is added to the second edition and references Letizia Álvarez de Toledo (a contemporary of Borges)? How has the editor come by this manuscript if they are outside the world of the library, or how have they gotten it to us if they are within? Their mention of the "twenty-two letters of the alphabet" and of the "*símbolos suficientes"* suggests that they are within its world and its ideology (but then, how do they even know of majuscules and digits?). Notice that Irby has taken the potentially unfaithful step of attributing the idea of sufficiency to the narrator. Di Giovanni does the same ("found to be sufficient by the unknown author"), Hurley is closer to the original ("sufficient symbols that our unknown author is referring to"), and Kerrigan is as usual the only one bold or timid enough for a literal translation ("sufficient symbols enumerated by the unknown author"). The irony inherent in this story, which claims 22 symbols should be enough to represent all possible language while simultaneously proving they are insufficient to express even this brief fiction, refutes any attribution of this idea of sufficiency to Borges. It rather seems that he has, as is customary, multiplied the layers and masks, creating a liminal figure who seems to bring Borges one step closer to the story's inside, while in truth shifting him yet one layer further away. And what to make of the "Borges" who signed a work of non-fiction two years earlier claiming the same idea that this fiction refutes or gently ironizes? Fictionalizing a seemingly non-fictional discourse while developing the truth in fiction is precisely the sort of deconstruction definitive of Borges's style.

The forbidden letters that appear within the library's texts, or at least on their spines (*dorso* — not, as Hurley would have it, their front covers), leave us with the most to ponder. It's easy to dismiss the editor's addition of capital letters in *Trueno peinado* and *El calambre de yeso* by mentally inserting the lower case letter, but what to make of *Axaxaxas mlö*? Should this be acsacsacsas, or ashashashas, or ajajajas? x is perhaps the most ironic letter for Borges to choose as irrelevant (as an "abbreviation"), given its regional and historical vicissitudes in Spanish pronunciation. At the very least, this reminds us that every sign and every letter is determined by a context to which it itself contributes — none can be removed or substituted losslessly. And it's easy enough to remove the umlaut, but why was it put there in the first place? We know that the phrase comes from an imagined language in Borges's "Tlön, Uqbar, Orbis Tertius," and means something like "onstreaming it mooned," but how does the editor know? Has that story been discovered inside the realm of the narrative (where Borges's "The Total Library" has clearly surfaced as well), and if so, is it read there as fiction or as encyclopedic? I'll hazard a few provisional indications of the endless paths a thorough interpretation of this intertextuality would have to follow: it adds yet another layer of complexity to the intricate fabric of Borges's work, as the phrase comes from a story where fiction and ideology continually intrude into the "real" world of the narrative (a transgression Gerard Genette would refer to as narrative metalepsis), and now intrudes on the world of another fiction. Furthermore, the idealism of Tlön exemplified by this phrase draws into question even the most basic assertion of identity, which is fundamental to the atomist claims of our narrator. Perhaps the two points of this umlaut (as well as its function) represent the very splitting of these atomic letters.

This insufficiency of the library's character set — that there will always be some characters left out of even the most capacious set, and that one or more characters can never substitute for others without some loss or gain — is what I referred to before as its accidental limitations. The essential insufficiency resides in the nature of a sign. Only if language has an atomic structure, if its letters and marks are indivisible, can the narrator's second axiom ("*The orthographical symbols are twenty-five in number*") be upheld. But the narrative itself draws into question the self-identity of these symbols, in the sentence immediately preceding:

> To perceive the distance between the divine and the human, it is enough to compare these crude wavering symbols which my fallible hand scrawls on the cover of a book, with the organic letters inside: punctual, delicate, perfectly black [*negrísimas*], inimitably symmetrical. (*Labyrinths* 52–53)

In order for divine and human writing to be distinguishable, the "twenty-five" symbols have to each be more or less than one in never being at one with themselves. Each is capable of separating from itself and being recognized as both the same and different, despite the narrator's dream of inimitability. A letter's lack of self-identity is the typographical version of the infinite divisibility of the atom, and it haunts even our narrator's attempt to secure and stabilize a structure of consistent signs (simple substances). Without this self-identity, the saturation of meaning is an essential impossibility, and the narrator's dream of totality is dependent on the symbols that subvert it.

Autobiography of Fiction

The irony by which the narrator's story undermines his own claims about the library's completeness leads us to the question of Borges's position in the text. Though this irony should forbid an identification of Borges with the narrator, we find several instances of autobiographical similarity between them. We must consider why and how Borges identifies himself with an ignorance that he necessarily transcends — a splitting that cannot surprise us too much from the author of "Borges and I."

To understand the autobiographical implications of a librarian hidden in the stacks scrawling a story he himself can barely read, we must consider Borges's life at the time of the story's composition. He recounts in "An Autobiographical Essay," which he dictated to Norman Thomas di Giovanni in English (*Autobiografía* 12), that in 1937, approaching age 40, he obtained his first full-time job at the Miguel Cané branch of the Municipal Library in Buenos Aires. He was assigned to work on a catalogue of the books, which no one seemed to need and was never to be completed. On his first day Borges indexed some four hundred books and was chastised by his coworkers. Their jobs depended on the incompletion of the catalogue, so they did as little work as possible — something Borges's diligence would expose. They instructed him to never index more than one hundred books, but to vary the amount from day to day to avoid suspicion. He spent the nine years he worked there doing an hour of cataloguing in the mornings, then passing the rest of the day hidden in the stacks reading and writing. One day he grazed his head on an open window casement and developed septicemia. He was expected to die, and when that did not come to pass his doctors predicted he would never regain his mental faculties. He was nervous to return to the writing of criticism or poetry, since he had a reputation in these fields and was just as worried to learn himself if he had lost his gift. It was sitting in this library (or, in warm weather, on the roof) and fearing for his capacities, that he wrote the stories of *El jardín de senderos que se bifurcan,* including "The Library of Babel."

It was also in his thirties that Borges began to lose his sight, so we can recognize his portrait in the librarian-narrator who writes, "now that my eyes can hardly decipher what I write, I am preparing to die just a few leagues from the hexagon in which I was born" (*Labyrinths* 52). It's likely that this shared blindness is intended as an emblem of the irony that leads us to identify Borges with this narrator, though this metaphor is certainly ableist. There are several other traces of Borges's life in this story. For example, here is his account of the minutely specific dimensions of the books:

> My Kafkian story "The Library of Babel" was meant as a nightmare version or magnification of that municipal library, and certain details in the text have no particular meaning. The numbers of books and shelves that I recorded in the story were literally what I had at my elbow. Clever critics have worried over those ciphers, and generously endowed them with mystic significance. ("Autobiographical Essay" 171).

It seems somewhat hard to believe, given the uniformity of the numbers in his short story:

> Each wall but one of each hexagon has five shelves; each shelf holds thirty-two books of a uniform size. Each book contains four hundred and ten pages; each page, forty lines; each line, eighty characters in black letter. (*Branching Paths* 76)

At the very least, we can recognize an emphasis on the number forty, biblical signifier of the endurance of long trials, and the temptation to interpret further remains. What is eschewed is precisely the effort toward realism and irregularity that counting lines and pages would produce — the only uncertainty acknowledged is in the number of characters per line: "*unas ochenta letras,*" or "some eighty letters." As is typical for Borges, the only realism occurs in the numbers we know to be false, those he varied with regularity to appease his coworkers at Miguel Cané.

There are also architectural details from his autobiographical essay that tie Borges's life to "The Library of Babel." He endows each of the hexagonal chambers of the story with a *zaguán* or narrow passage, which we learn was part of the architecture of the home in which he was born: "Like most of the houses of that day, it had a flat roof; a long, arched entranceway, called a *zaguán*" ("Autobiographical Essay" 135). It is this same home to which Borges traces an important recollection: "If I were asked to name the chief event in my life, I should say my father's library. In fact, I sometimes think I have never strayed outside that library" (140). If the present essay has an aim, it is to universalize this condition Borges traces to the accidents of his childhood and his bookish nature. That his life repeated certain scenes, that he went from this childhood library to Miguel Cané, which became in his imagination the inescapable Library of Babel, and that he went on to become the third blind head librarian of the National Library of Buenos Aires, makes him a fitting prophet of generalized textuality, though the latter does not depend on such a life story.

What Borges attributes to his biography in his non-fiction, we can find universalized in his fiction. In his autobiographical essay, he writes: "This endless distance, I found out, was called the pampa, and when I learned that the farmhands were gauchos, like the characters in Eduardo Gutiérrez, that gave them a certain glamor. I have always come to things after coming to books" ("Autobiographical Essay" 143). That language or textuality precedes experience is implicit in the narrative of "The Library of Babel." Our narrator expresses as much when he says that "to speak is to fall into tautology" (*Labyrinths* 57). So, though Borges and his more careful readers can take an ironic distance from the narrator's claims of the self-identity of the letter and the infinity of his universe, we should recognize that it is not as easy as uttering a negation to take leave of these theses. The act of recognition that precedes our consciousness of every sign and thing (and undermines any supposed difference between language and reality) creates a unity even as it divides a thing from itself.[9] For this reason Borges places himself on both sides of the narrative he creates, as its pompous and deluded narrator as much as its presumably demystified author. We can account for his public persona in this way as well; his relentless humility and self-deprecation is perhaps an expression of feeling both less vain than and inadequate next to — Borges.

The last autobiographical moment appears in the story's final footnote, which records an observation attributed to Letizia Álvarez de Toledo. Given that the note only appeared in the second edition, and that Toledo was an Argentine author and part of Borges's social circle, it's entirely possible that the note records a comment of hers made in response to Borges's story. Her observation is as follows: "this vast library is useless. Rigorously speaking, *a single volume* would be sufficient, a volume of ordinary format, printed in nine or ten point type, containing an infinite number of infinitely thin leaves" (Borges, *Labyrinths* 58). Twenty years later, Borges returned to the idea of this footnote when he composed "The Book of Sand," a first-person narrative whose narrator admits to working in the Argentine National Library before retirement, and who begins his account by promising, "To claim that it is true is nowadays the convention of every made-up story. Mine, however, *is* true." (87). This narrator purchases a book with never-ending pages from a traveling salesman who heard it called the book of sand because, "nei-

---

9 These propositions may appear dogmatic or obscure at this point, but they are considered more patiently in the next chapter.

ther the book nor the sand has any beginning or end" (89).[10] We should recall, from "The Two Kings and Their Two Labyrinths," that endless sand is recognized by Borges as one form the labyrinth may take, as it is in its own way inescapable. It is precisely this quicksand that our narrator finds himself sinking deeper within, and which I would surmise he shares in common with Borges the author. His poignant recollection that, "in the meagre intervals my insomnia granted, I dreamed of the book" ("Book of Sand" 91), recalls a nightmare in which Borges the labyrinth-maker found himself trapped, trapped in his dream and in its repetitions:

> I have the nightmare every other night. The pattern is always the same. I find myself, let's say, always on a street corner in Buenos Aires, or in a room, quite an ordinary room, and then I attempt another street corner and another room and they are the same. That goes on and on. Then I say to myself, well, this is the nightmare of the labyrinth. I merely have to wait, and I wake up in due time. But sometimes I dream I wake up and find myself on the same street corner, in the same room, or in the same marshland, ringed in by the same fog or looking into the same mirror — and then I know that I am not really awake. I go on dreaming until I wake, but the nightmare feeling lasts for two minutes, perhaps, until I feel that I am going mad. Then suddenly all that vanishes. I can go back to sleep. (*Borges at 80* n.p.)

I sense Borges lost in a textual labyrinth, partly of his own creation, though partly preceding him and universally inescapable, when I read the weary narrator of this later story. When he returns to the National Library to "hide a leaf [...] in a forest," leaving the book of sand on a shelf while attempting not to notice which one, he is trying, feebly, to exorcise this old ghost (Borges,

---

10 While we can recognize its continuities with the book of Borges's footnote, the book of sand also contains illustrations and varying scripts, either promising or eluding totality in any number of dimensions.

"Book of Sand" 91). But this "I" has no power over the Borges who precedes him and his creations, even if they are identical.

The Cult of Books

In "Tlön, Uqbar, Orbis Tertius," Borges imagined a world where common sense aligned with idealist philosophy, a perfect inversion of the materialism that underlies our average experience. "The Library of Babel" is another example of his skill to perfectly invert a fundamental binary, in this case the distinction between invention and discovery. We are used to thinking of ourselves as free subjects, and our thoughts, speech, and actions as expressions of our spontaneity, thus as original acts or inventions. It is manifest for the librarians that their use of language can only repeat permutations existing within the library, and thus they think of their own creations as inferior to the divinely authored texts they imitate. While we celebrate originality and have a legal system established to recognize invention, they place greater value on the discovery or finding of preexisting text. From the deconstruction of invention and discovery, and the universal library that conditions it,[11] follow the instability of all the most fundamental binary oppositions shaping thought.

In "On the Cult of Books," Borges traces the elevation of writing to sacred status, the culmination of which he finds in the Christian tradition of the two scriptures. God created two books, according to this way of thought, the Bible and nature. Both must be studied to learn God's will. In "The Library of Babel," we witness an almost parodistic literalization of this metaphor — nature is, if not a book, at least a library. Indeed, our narrator seeks out just as much meaning in its *dotación* (endowment) of shelves, hexagons, and latrines as in its pages. Still, an inversion takes place that allows what we think of as cultural ar-

---

11 In the chapter that follows, we will see how the derivative or repetitive status of language is not a product of the existence of a universal library (as we have seen already, even in Borges's story, the library is never purely universal), but rather a principle belonging to the essence of language.

tifact to attain a natural status, and thus proximity to the divine will (for the religiously inclined). The problems that face a finite mind attempting to grasp the infinite merely shift as a result. For example, "Those who judge it [the world] to be limited postulate that in remote places the corridors and stairways and hexagons can [in]conceivably come to an end — which is absurd" (Borges, *Labyrinths* 58). We know that this question plagued ancient philosophers and continues to cause controversy among contemporary physicists. A problem that plays itself out for us in terms of relativistic space-time or the multiverse runs up against the same non-limit for the librarian in terms of the basic structural units of his universe. Furthermore, as we know from the traditions in our world that consider certain texts divinely inspired or created, this provenance makes their interpretation no more certain or secure. The vast realm of allegorical and cryptographic possibilities that offer themselves to the librarians searching for the truth of the divine word have their closest parallel in the Cabbalistic tradition that fascinated Borges as well.

Because our narrator thinks of all text as already created and originating from God, the tasks of authorship and reading are transformed. Recalling the difficulty of finding intelligibility among the library's volumes, our narrator writes, "A blasphemous sect suggested that all searches be given up and that men everywhere shuffle letters and symbols until they succeeded in composing, by means of an improbable stroke of luck, the canonical books" (*Ficciones* 84). What he refers to as "shuffling letters" we call writing, and this inversion, like all those carried out by Borges's fiction, reveals something fundamental that applies equally to our own existence. We too are dependent on the preexistence of language, both letters and words, and by necessity our every composition is a sort of found text. Every writer knows that her product never quite corresponds to its idea or ideal, and that the process of writing is just as likely to produce a surplus of meaning as a loss. The Truth, on the other hand, is more impossible than improbable.

The task of reading undergoes a related transformation. Our narrator describes a "regressive" method for locating a desired book: "To locate book A, consult first a book B which indicates A's position; to locate book B, consult first a book C, and so on to infinity...." (*Labyrinths* 56). We scholars may immediately sense the parody and absurdity of the task of criticism implicit in these lines — whether our search for meaning in a text progresses "regressively" through its history of interpretation and an author's influences, or progressively through the writing of ideas that are our "own" (of course this designation is insufficient), we know that our task does not end when the truth is reached, but when exhaustion sets in. There is always a lost, hidden, forgotten, or yet to be written link to be added to this chain, though never a final seal.

Many readers and critics associate these inverted worlds with fantasy writing and/or with the philosophical systems implicitly motivating them. Some draw the unjustified conclusion that Borges therefore was not concerned with more mundane and local realities, such as Argentine politics. The worst abuses of logic come from those who assume that because Borges wrote what they consider science fiction or fantasy, or because he read philosophy and spent time in libraries, or because he had an imagination or life of the mind at all, he therefore was denigrating the public person and reality. Take for example this comment from Clive James, reaffirming a statement of Borges's contemporary Ernesto Sábato: "Borges did fear the bitterness of reality, and he did take refuge in an invented world" ("Bad Politics").[12]

---

12   Jaime Alazraki also posits that literature, philosophy, and metafiction represent an escape from "the world" — "Borges has made a similar choice: confronted with the chaos of the world, he has chosen the order of the library, the safety of a decipherable labyrinth [...]. He wrote fiction based on theologies and philosophies, literature founded in literature. He knew that the hard face of reality lurks in every corner of life, but he renounced the world, because, he said, of its impenetrable nature. Instead he anchored his writings in the order of the intellect, in the chartable waters of the library" (182–83). It is remarkable for a lifelong reader of Borges to come away from his work with the feeling that it is a simple matter to divide world from text, or that either the intellect or the library are orderly or "chartable."
     In no way are Borges's creations safer or more decipherable than "reality" — nor are they less so. One does not take leave of the world by writing

I take issue not with criticism of Borges's indefensible politics, but with the notion that a capacity for abstraction was somehow to blame. Gina Apostol has offered one of the most nuanced and intriguing readings of Borges I have encountered, the matrix of an indefinite number of possible interpretations of the political and postcolonial themes in Borges's work. In response to critics' tendency to read Borges as apolitical because of his penchant for fiction and metafiction, she develops an elegant theory of the condition of postcolonial life as living within another's fantasy.[13] Consider the protagonist of "The Circular Ruins," who tries to dream a man into existence, only to learn he is a dream himself, or the narrator of "Tlön, Uqbar, Orbis Tertius," who learns

---

literature or even literature about literature. *Reality is a metafiction.* Who could possibly take a serious look at politics today (so to speak) and come away with the conclusion that its primary impetus is reality? Living inside the fantasy of a madman is the condition of Borges's characters—and it is our condition as well. Far from fleeing it, one's only hope of confronting this situation, learning how our world is put together and how to take it apart or build it differently comes from the construction and analysis of metafiction.

Borges also showed us the double-edged nature of this political imaginary. One can weave the veil of reality (behind which are only other veils, or nothing at all) for the sake of the best — or the worst. And the condemnation Alazraki and others offer of literature and philosophy is ultimately a defense of Borges's worst political commitments. He did not flee political commitment by writing but became a token man of letters on the side of his nation's autocrats. Borges's supposed European or cosmopolitan sympathies must be understood in light of the following (which is, again, double-edged — both the effacement and apotheosis of nationalism): "Gibbon observes that in the Arab book par excellence, the Koran, there are no camels; I believe that if there were ever any doubt as to the authenticity of the Koran, this lack of camels would suffice to prove that it is Arab. It was written by Mohammed, and Mohammed, as an Arab, had no reason to know that camels were particularly Arab; they were, for him, a part of reality, and he had no reason to single them out, while the first thing a forger, a tourist, or an Arab nationalist would do is bring on the camels, whole caravans of camels on every page; but Mohammed, as an Arab, was unconcerned; he knew he could be Arab without camels. I believe that we Argentines can be like Mohammed; we can believe in the possibility of being Argentine without abounding in local color" ("Argentine Writer" 424).

13 In *Out of Context,* Daniel Balderston also traces the intricate interweaving of history and politics in Borges's stories.

that the ideology that ultimately overtakes his society is "a hoax underwritten by some crass American millionaire" (Apostol). Following Apostol's lead, we can indicate the trailhead of a post-colonial reading of "The Library of Babel," where a species of men finds itself in an inescapable textual universe and attempts to create its own culture and religion out of the elements it has inherited. Again, we see that the inversion of nature and culture in Borges's work does not separate it from our reality but opens a perspective distorted by the classical interpretation or domi-nant discourse. We should add to our reading of the narrator's blind spots how a certain locality or finitude always disrupts the universalizing aspiration, and should re-read all of Borges's complex and self-contradictory statements on cosmopolitanism in light of this persistent irony.

Our consideration of the inversion of binaries could not be complete without touching on the genus or genre of gender. Though it is never said outright, this race of librarians seems ex-clusively male — referenced either with masculine terms ("Like all men of the Library" [Labyrinths 52], "All men felt themselves to be the masters" [55]) or abstract terms such as "the human species" (58).[14] It seems necessary to relate this gender approach-ing genderlessness with the general lack of the bodily in this universe, where there are generations without any mention of reproduction, and "faecal necessities" without any evidence of food (Branching Paths 73). Our narrator's dream of dissolving in the infinite air seems to be another dream of bodilessness.[15] This

---

14 The only exception is the name of Letizia Álvarez de Toledo, which appears at a liminal point where the narrative crosses into another dimension, and where it describes the invaginated structure of a book always containing another internal fold.

15 The narrator's fear of extinction, lament of a fallen humanity, expresses it-self in an interestingly ambiguous phrase. While "La especia humana — la única," becomes "the human species — the unique species" for Irby, "the human species — the only species" for Hurley, and "the human race — the only race" for di Giovanni, Kerrigan is an outlier, shifting the application of the adjective unique: "the human species — the unique human species" (87). In other words, Kerrigan offers the possible reading that humanity is differ-ent from other species, rather than the only one. His interpretation seems

uniformity is inevitably double-edged. On the one hand, it plays into a tradition of the scholar, philosopher, and man of reason just as much as the religious mystic or fantastic journeyer who transcends the limits of the individual as an exclusively male role. On the other hand, it must be read in the context of a narrative where every dream of unity and universality is disrupted by its narrator's oversights and errors, as a reminder that humanity as a fulcrum of life and spirit is impossible without the difference-from-self of gender.

Branching Libraries

Let us return to the library of Borges's childhood, the one he claimed never to have left. One has the sense, reading through his impressively erudite non-fiction, that the world he inhabits is in fact made up of that library, and likely a few others as well, and that he guides us through his world by flipping its pages. We find, in "The Library of Babel," references to many of the figures who dominate his non-fiction. Each of these references leads us to another gap, aporia, or representation of what cannot be represented in language.

Most of these references come in the enumerations from both "The Total Library" and "The Library of Babel," which list a small and curious subset meant to give an impression of the breadth of the full collection. In the former, it reads as follows:

> Everything would be in its blind volumes. Everything: the detailed history of the future, Aeschylus' *The Egyptians,* the exact number of times that the waters of the Ganges have reflected the flight of a falcon, the secret and true name of Rome, the encyclopedia Novalis would have constructed,

---

less defensible than the one chosen by the other three, and perhaps more of a protest or self-defense in the face of the organic absurdity of the story. It is more in keeping with the narrative to see humanity, and possibly men, as the only living things in this library without bookworms, which we could read as an expression of both phallogocentrism and carnophallogocentrism, while always harboring their potential deconstruction.

my dreams and half-dreams at dawn on August 14, 1934, the proof of Pierre Fermat's theorem, the unwritten chapters of *Edwin Drood,* those same chapters translated into the language spoken by the Garamantes, the paradoxes Berkeley invented concerning Time but didn't publish, Urizen's books of iron, the premature epiphanies of Stephen Dedalus, which would be meaningless before a cycle of a thousand years, the Gnostic Gospel of Basilides, the song the sirens sang, the complete catalog of the Library, the proof of the inaccuracy of that catalog. (216)

"The Library of Babel" alters this list somewhat:

[I]ts bookshelves contain all possible combinations of the twenty-two orthographic symbols (a number which, though unimaginably vast, is not infinite) — that is, all that is able to be expressed, in every language. *All* — the detailed history of the future, the autobiographies of the archangels, the faithful catalog of the Library, thousands and thousands of false catalogs, the proof of the falsity of those false catalogs, a proof of the falsity of the *true* catalog, the gnostic gospel of Basilides, the commentary upon that gospel, the commentary on the commentary on that gospel, the true story of your death, the translation of every book into every language, the interpolations of every book into all books, the treatise Bede could have written (but did not) on the mythology of the Saxon people, the lost books of Tacitus. (*Complete Fictions* 115)

Several forms of impossibility are implicit in these lists. For example, while "the proof of Pierre Fermat's theorem" could have been checked if it were found (even in 1939, before a proof existed — in a limited sense of existence), unwritten works of literature ("the missing chapters of *Edwin Drood*"), philosophy ("the paradoxes Berkeley invented concerning time but didn't publish"), and history ('the treatise Bede could have written (but did not) on the mythology of the Saxon people") would be unidentifiable — though each presents quite different possibilities for expert verification. The works have wildly differing ontological statuses, from works written and lost, to works unwritten but imagined by once living people, to works imagined to belong to fictional characters ("the premature epiphanies of Stephen Dedalus, which would be meaningless before a cycle of a thousand years"). While "the complete catalog of the Library" is impossible, "the proof of the inaccuracy of that catalog" would not be. "The song the sirens sang" could seduce any one of its listeners — would each of us find it in a different book, or could we find a single book with this Protean property? As Ana María Barrenechea says of a similar enumeration in "The Aleph" (Barrenechea 86), this list combines the universal ("a minute history of the future") and the particular ("the true story of your death"). Impossibilities abound within each of the referenced texts as well.

"The archangels' autobiographies," mentioned in "The Library of Babel" (*Labyrinths* 54), "the secret and true name of Rome," mentioned in "The Total Library" (216), and "the Gnostic Gospel of Basilides," mentioned in both, all are referenced in Borges's non-fiction, and each has resonances of the unrepresentable divine name. "A History of Angels" lists the properties ascribed to angels by a theological tradition that attempted to make them greater than man but less than God. Each attribute approaches immateriality and eternity, and the most interesting for our purposes is "the power of conversing among themselves instantaneously without [*sin apelar a*] words or signs" (17). Once we are forced to recognize, as we have been by "The Library of Babel," that the sign or word is an ineluctable part of our experience, how could this autobiography be communicated to us, other than by paradox and apophasis, like the phrase "conversation without signs"? "A Defense of Basilides the False" describes a vision that would not have been out of place in "Kafka and his Precursors," a God who created 365 mutually subordinate heavens, before arriving at the divinity we know from the scriptures as creator of heaven and earth. We pass through all realms to the highest heaven only by knowing the secret names of these divinities. "A History of the Echoes of a Name" discusses the name of

God as well and recounts "that the true name of Rome was also secret." This essay describes God's revelation or dissimulation of his name to Moses, "I AM THAT I AM," as the perfect cipher or name of names. While the speculative philosophers would say that this named the unity of existence and essence, it was just as true when Swift, having lost his mind, was heard repeating, "I am that I am, I am that I am…." (407). The name that is true, the absolute and final Word about any existing thing, cannot be revealed to finite ears for essential reasons — thus it remains secret or hidden. Nor will they appear among the universal library's pages — again, for essential reasons.

Most curiously, Borges chooses to cite himself in the story, and to let himself be thoroughly ridiculed. The unattributed quotation that prompts some of our narrator's most eloquent defenses of the library is nearly matched by the final words of "The Total Library." Their appearance in "The Library of Babel" reads as follows:

> The impious maintain that nonsense is normal in the Library and that the reasonable (and even humble and pure coherence) is an almost miraculous exception. They speak (I know) of the "feverish Library whose chance volumes are constantly in danger of changing into others and affirm, negate, and confuse everything like a delirious divinity." These words, which not only denounce the disorder but exemplify it as well, notoriously prove their authors' [*su*] abominable taste and desperate ignorance.[16] (*Labyrinths* 57)

One is reminded of Borges's confession that "I have even secretly longed to write, under a pen name, a merciless tirade against myself" ("Autobiographical Essay" 185). Uncertainties abound. First, I have never been able to tell if Borges meant his words in "The Total Library" to refer to the universal library he was describing, or to a separate nightmare structure whose books

---

16 It is only by ignoring several layers of irony that some critics manage placidly to cite this passage as an example of "chaos" in Borges's work.

would literally have letters that shifted and changed before a reader's eyes. If he speaks of the universal library, the "danger of changing into others" must refer to something like the necessity of interpretation. Furthermore, we are again in a situation (as with the character set) where Borges's non-fiction is being drawn into question by his fiction, but here it is our often fallible narrator who questions it. Do these two negations produce an affirmation? Our narrator specifies his objection: "In truth, the Library includes all verbal structures [...] but not a single example of absolute nonsense" (*Labyrinths* 57). But the passage cited makes no mention of nonsense. In order to "affirm, negate," or even "confuse," they must make some form of sense. It seems to me that the ultimate point of contention comes down to the narrator's desire to celebrate his universe. If one writer (Borges) speaks of the monstrous indifference and superfluity of its contents, another writer (Borges?) will celebrate its copious potential.

Should the library be celebrated or reviled? Perhaps another of its texts can help us to understand the relation of this valorization to repetition, novelty, and temporality. The narrator recounts a book of pure gibberish, except for the phrase "*Oh tiempo tus pirámides*" on its second-to-last page. Irby and Hurley translate this as "Oh time, thy pyramids," using the elevated pronoun presumably because they recognize the reference to Shakespeare's Sonnet 123. In the precursor poem, time's pyramids refer to everything that comes to be and passes away in time, belying the profound permanence underneath:

> No! Time, thou shalt not boast that I do change:
> Thy pyramids built up with newer might
> To me are nothing novel, nothing strange;
> They are but dressings of a former sight.

In this sonnet, the persona's concluding disavowal of time's purported novelty, in order to "be true" to the underlying permanence, represents a faith in God beyond this world of apparitions. Borges, when he borrows this figure, allows it to transform, despite any seeming repetition in his gesture. In addition to its appearance in "The Library of Babel," time's pyramids arise in a later poem, "Of Heaven and Hell." While this poem also posits something divine underlying temporality and its contents, the divine is by no means unitary:

> In the clear glass of a dream, I have glimpsed
> the Heaven and Hell that lie in wait for us [*prometidos*]:
> when Judgement Day sounds in the last trumpets
> and planet and millennium [*el planeta milenario*] both
> disintegrate, and all at once, O Time,
> all your ephemeral pyramids cease to be,
> the colors and the lines that trace the past
> will in the semi-darkness form a face,
> a sleeping face, faithful, still, unchangeable
> (the face of the loved one, or, perhaps, your own)
> and the sheer contemplation of that face —
> never-changing, whole, beyond corruption —
> will be, for the rejected, an Inferno,
> and, for the elected, Paradise. (*Poems of the Night* 51)

Borges borrows this idea from Swedenborg, that there is only one final destination, but it is an unbearable hell for corrupted souls, and a paradise for the elect. Now, the "Borges" who wrote "The Total Library," who may or may not be the same author that ironized the opinions he expressed there in his short story and several later essays, compares the universal library to Hell:

> One of the habits of the mind is the invention of horrible imaginings. The mind has invented Hell, it has invented predestination to Hell, it has imagined [...] masks, mirrors, operas, the teratological Trinity: the Father, the Son, and the unresolvable Ghost, articulated into a single organism.... I have tried to rescue from oblivion a subaltern horror: the vast, contradictory Library. (216)

Of course, as we just saw, the narrator of "The Library of Babel" ridicules this opinion and celebrates the vastness of the creation he inhabits. The narrator has the more Shakespearean view of a divine mind and will underlying the seeming chaos of the library, ultimately guaranteeing its meaning and purpose. But perhaps there is another destiny or destination, within this same structure, one that does not depend on totalization in order to redeem what appears fallen or finite. Rather than lamenting or cursing the dissemination of meaning in so many unstable texts, could this not be the source of liberation and play, for a reader unencumbered by truth and falsehood? Perhaps the change in register, from Shakespeare's rejection (No! Time…) to Borges's more wistful "Oh time…," represents this reconciliation to its ephemeral creations. As though to say, "Oh time, I know you're nothing, but your pyramids…."

While we could continue endlessly, finding the traces of any predecessor or epigone in this library that contains all textuality, even those still to come, we will finish with a reference to the whole. In one of his many passages affirming the infinity of the library, our narrator writes, "Let it suffice now for me to repeat the classic dictum: *The Library is a sphere whose exact center is any one of its hexagons and whose circumference is inaccessible*" (*Labyrinths* 52). In his essay "Pascal's Sphere," Borges finds an almost identical phrase in a series of authors nearly coterminous with the textual record. Said alternately of God, the universe, or nature, under Pascal's pen it became "Nature is an infinite sphere, the center of which is everywhere, the circumference nowhere" ("Sphere" 353). Noting that a medieval tradition used this formula to celebrate God's immanence and transcendence and that an early modern tradition used it to celebrate the perfectibility of human knowledge, he finds a marked shift in Pascal who hesitated when calling it "frightful." Pascal, we know, reacted against the scientism of Descartes and the application of a geometrical method to philosophy — the *mathesis universalis*. This method, which pretended to be an unshakeable ground (*fundamentum inconcussum*) for absolute knowledge of the absolute, was criticized by the nonetheless faithful Pascal, who felt the longing and uncertainty of the finitude of knowledge. Not knowing how it began or how it would end, this center ignorant of its extremities expressed itself with the model of the infinite sphere. Representing the library from the viewpoint of finite experience is what separates Borges from his predecessors like Lasswitz, who merely imagined its extent. The desire for infinity, vindication, and justification that obsesses our narrator is just this desire for an absolute ground, an access to the infinite that could anchor and secure all finite judgments. When he prays to an unknown God that some librarian encounter a total book — a complete catalog of the library — he is longing at least for the possibility of this ground: "Let me be outraged and annihilated [i.e., finite], but for one instant, in one being, let Your enormous Library be justified" (*Labyrinths* 57). The impossibility of this catalog is what we must consider in conclusion.

Babel

We may have traveled far enough now to gain a vantage point for a glance back, to try to ask a question about the title that both affirms by its presence the unity of its contents and draws the same into question by placing us in Babel. But how far back or forward must one step to glimpse totality?[17] The question of Babel, both as tower and as library, is precisely one of totality or unity — is it possible for humanity to share a common language? Is it as simple as finding a unitary structure (which, as we have already seen, the library is not)? The story of Babel poses the question of whether human beings can ever give

---

17 Everything contained in these pages could be seen as a useless and wordy elaboration of Paul de Man's "A Modern Master," where the constant theme of villainy, revelation, and betrayal in Borges's work is interpreted as a representation of the necessary perfidy of the artist, whose task is to supplement existence with the simulacrum of totality in the form of art. One is reminded of de Man's statement about Nietzsche's word: "'Only as an aesthetic phenomenon is existence and the world forever justified:' the famous quotation, twice repeated in *The Birth of Tragedy,* should not be taken too serenely, for it is an indictment of existence rather than a panegyric of art" (*Allegories* 93).

a name to themselves as a sovereign, autonomous, intentional act, or whether we must receive language from a more powerful source, and receive it as a burden, a punishment, and a debt. The title, "The Library of Babel," presents the same problem: a name that never recurs within the text, and that appears in both its first and second printing in all majuscules, as though not a single letter belonged to the universe of the narration, it leaves us to wonder whether it came from inside the story's world, or whether it was imposed from outside, as though by a jealous God.

In the Bible, the task of building the tower of Babel develops from a desire for unity: "Come, let us build ourselves a city, and a tower with its top in the heavens, and let us make a name for ourselves; otherwise we shall be scattered abroad upon the face of the whole earth" (Gen. 11.4). Creating a name for themselves means many things: they will not be scattered — that is, their familiars and descendants will have a single home and retain their single name, and this unity will have its symbol in an edifice that is one and unites them all. An edifice that reaches to heaven. God prevents this not only by stopping their construction, but by giving them a name of his own:

> And the Lord said, "Look, they are one people, and they have all one language; and this is only the beginning of what they will do; nothing that they propose to do will now be impossible for them. Come, let us go down, and confuse their language there, so that they will not understand one another's speech." So the Lord scattered them abroad from there over the face of all the earth, and they left off building the city. Therefore it was called Babel, because there the Lord confused the language of all the earth; and from there the Lord scattered them abroad over the face of all the earth. (Gen. 11.6–9).

Only the infinite, God, can give Himself a name, and a name that would be one. As we have seen, that name remains secret from his creatures. We must receive our names, and they can never be univocal, as the example of Babel shows. As Derrida explains in "Des Tours de Babel," the name received is both a proper name, a mark without a corresponding concept, thus untranslatable, and a common noun meaning confusion (109). Thus it both refuses translation (though the English homophones Babel/babble come very close to doing it justice), and demands translation, even within its source language. One has to explain, to put two or more words in place of one, in order to "translate" this "within" a language or between two languages. We can thus take it as an example of the impossibility of identifying a language as one, single, or unitary. It models and enacts the fate of humanity after Babel, for whom God "*at the same time* imposes and forbids translation" (Derrida, "Babel" 108). The Library of Babel presents the same condition, where translation or the crossing of borders — for example from the finite to the infinite — is both necessary and impossible.

The librarians of our story find themselves within a continuous (though, as we saw, never single) architecture whose spiral extends endlessly — are they then in a completed tower of Babel? But Borges shows us that the unity of language and genealogy thus implied is impossible for essential reasons, not merely on account of the whims of a jealous God. The sects and dialects that appear among the librarians and within their internally diverse texts attest to the impossibility of this unity. Our narrator informs us that linguistic difference has inflected the interpretation of the library's texts, in a passage that gives echoes of another Babelian fiction, Kafka's "The Great Wall of China:"

[T]he most ancient men, the first librarians, used a language quite different from the one we now speak; it is true that a few miles to the right the tongue is dialectical and that ninety floors farther up, it is incomprehensible. (*Labyrinths* 53)

These differences and this *confusion* can occur, as we know, between speakers of "the same" language or dialect, and thus every language has internal division or difference. In a parenthetical aside added to the second edition, our narrator explores the impossibility of securing the unity of a language:

> An *n* number of possible languages use the same vocabulary; in some of them, the symbol *library* allows the correct definition *a ubiquitous and lasting system of hexagonal galleries,* but *library* is *bread* or *pyramid* or anything else, and these seven words[18] which define it have another value. You who read me, are you sure of understanding my language? (57–58)

Of course, we note immediately that his definition of *library* differs from ours, and that his understanding of bread and pyramid remains uncertain, given the absence of food in his universe and the stated impossibility of the triangle. Even "the same" words, without a single mark to set them apart, can contain, admit, or enable a nonfinite number of languages. Our narrator's only mistake is in attributing this to the library's totality, in thinking that it could somehow contain "all" languages.

Religion unites the librarians no better than language. The Inquisitors, Purifiers, and those who seek the Man of the Book have disagreements about the proper use, interpretation, and respect of the library that are never merely doctrinal, as the story's several references to violent death make clear. What each sect struggles against is the dispersion or dissemination of meaning. In place of the scattering of multiple books, "The mystics claim that their ecstasy reveals to them a circular chamber containing a great circular book, whose spine is continuous and which follows the complete circle of the walls [...]. This cyclical book is God" (52). A single, uninterrupted book in a single, complete room is the vision of the longed-for truth that contrasts with the one hidden among endless shelves and volumes. The Purifiers had the impossible hope of destroying books until they reached "the books in the Crimson Hexagon: books whose format is

---

18 Seven in the original — Irby has used eight words to translate them, adding the initial article. He is also the dyscalculic translator who placed 35 books on each of the library's shelves.

smaller than usual [*que los naturales*], all-powerful, illustrated and magical" (Borges, *Labyrinths* 56). A strange reference — this uniquely colored hexagon could refer to the process of miniating, and thus these "illustrated" manuscripts would also be "smaller than usual" — miniature. One might try to draw out a reference to some of Borges's favorite literature — *The Dream of the Red Chamber* or "The Masque of the Red Death." Regardless, we can recognize a desire analogous to that of the mystics, to discover a book or books that would be set apart, that one would see at a glance to be special and the force of whose truth would overwhelm us ("all-powerful," "magical") without recourse to lengthy interpretation.

The most problematic and revealing of these sects is the one seeking the Man of the Book, the librarian who would have found and read the library's master catalogue, and thus would be omniscient. We should consider, in refuting this belief, not its improbability but its impossibility. What would constitute a master catalogue? What would it look like, and how would one know one had found it? As our narrator has taught us, one can never dismiss a book as meaningless, and any text can be given any meaning allegorically or cryptographically. How, for example, would the librarian's "wordy and useless epistle" be classified? As fiction or philosophy, fantasy or autobiography? Is its theme infinity or inescapable finitude? The same problem facing Barrenechea (see n. 5, above) in devising categories to contain mutable and undecidable symbols faces any librarian (in this story or outside it) trying to separate a true catalogue or predicate from a false one. Borges examined the same impossibility in his famous essay on "John Wilkins' Analytical Language." Wilkins dreamed of constructing a language where every letter would be motivated or have a meaning — for example — "*a* means animal; *ab,* mammalian; *abo,* carnivorous; *aboj,* feline; *aboje,* cat; *abi,* herbivorous; *abiv,* equine; etc." (230). Such a language is only possible if our conceptual structure is absolute, and thus evades us in the here-below. For those of us still disseminating like the seed or shards of the scattered Babelians,

"there is no universe in the organic, unifying sense of that ambiguous word" (231).

Non-Fiction?

I was contemplating "The Library of Babel" one night, considering how it treats language as a purely mechanical, combinatorial process, and thought — that would make a killer app. I created a website, libraryofbabel.info, that currently contains every possible page of 3,200 characters, using a character set of the twenty-six lower case letters, space, comma, and period. It has received some attention from the press, who tend to frame its existence as though technology has now made possible the reality of something that was previously only a fantasy. For example, the following appeared in a *Slate* article entitled, "Jorge Luis Borges' 'Library of Babel' Is Now a Real Website. Borges Would Be Alarmed:" "But still: Borges intended his story to be ironic — haunting because it was impossible — so he would surely be alarmed to know we've moved a bit closer to its realization." I remain skeptical of this interpretation that seems an outgrowth of the mystification of technology in our culture. As we considered in the previous chapter, Borges's library failed to live up to its universal pretensions for essential, not accidental reasons (thus, libraryofbabel.info falls short as well). It's also the case that the property of iterability or repeatability, belonging to or disrupting the essence of language, is what makes possible both his short story and the website. We will now turn to a consideration of this essence or non-essence of language as it reveals itself in Borges's story, in its virtual avatar, and in the ever transforming contexts language both enables and subverts.

What would it mean for the universal library to exist? It was imagined as a container of all possible expression, a totality that nonetheless defies possibility. What should we make, then, of the effect it has on users? Borges's librarians thought that they could only interact with language in the modes of repetition and discovery — invention was denied to them by the omniferousness of their library. Visitors to libraryofbabel.info often reach a similar conclusion about the deconstruction of the distinction between invention and discovery, saying that now everything has been written, that language is henceforth possible without us, and that I hold the copyright on every previously unwritten page of text, while also having violated every existing copyright. But language does not become repetition as a result of the exhaustion of possibility (something essentially forbidden); rather, iterability resides at its origin.

This principle is most visible when we witness our every possible thought, speech, or writing reproduced mechanically, without recourse to the intentions of an author. We should recognize not that some machine or program has displaced our intentions and their former necessity, but rather that language was always possible without us. Iterability is this capacity of anything that functions like a sign to be wrested from its motivating context, to replace its speaker, its recipient, and its referent for another or for none at all. This is an essential property of a signifier — to function as such, it must be recognizable in different contexts, from this or that speaker, in speech or writing, in different tones of voice, in different typefaces, from man or woman, etc. Still, we should not be seduced by the dream of philosophers, that a sign corresponds to a pure and separate meaning, eternal and unchanging, independent of the forms its expression takes. This language of the angels, communicating itself immediately to thought without signs, would allow for the saturation of possible expression were it itself possible. But the gesture toward the infinite that we make in recognizing and identifying different signs, like the tremulous handwriting of our narrator and the symmetrical writing of God, always straddles this divide, carrying with it some meaning from the context it is departing.

As Derrida says, marks remain "separable from their internal and external context and also from themselves, inasmuch as the very iterability which constituted their identity does not permit them ever to be a unity that is identical to itself" ("Signature Event Context" 10). Nor can we control a sign by constraining its context — the potential for context is inexhaustible, even if or perhaps because context in general is ineluctable.

For anything to function like a sign or mark, it must have this property of iterability, which means that for us to speak or write at all, we must express ourselves with signs that remain mechanically reproducible, and capable of citation, parody, etc. If language were somehow tied to its motivating context and literal reference, everything that departs from this, like imagination, irony, fiction, lies, and so on, would be impossible. Borges's short story is thus not one among others, but the story of all literature, and with it all reality. This or that universal library, mine or Borges's, may have its limits and constraints, but everything in principle sits on the shelf of the universal library that resides in the essence of language.

Of libraryofbabel.info, That It Perhaps Does Not Exist

Given its character set and dimensions, libraryofbabel.info contains $29^{3,200}$ unique pages, or about $10^{4,677}$. In comparison, the universe contains only 10^{80} atoms. It would require many universes of hard drives to store all its pages on disk. This raises some necessary questions about the possibility or actuality of its existence. In considering the algorithm used to circumvent this impossibility, our focus will be on raising the question of the virtual archive and how it complicates our notion of presence and absence.

When I first constructed the website, I stored randomly generated text files on disk because my programming skills were not sophisticated enough to do anything more complex. Every URL for a page of text contained the name of a text file on my computer, and when a page of text was requested, the server opened that file, retrieved the text, and sent it to the client. After generating one million text files, my hard drive was full, and I had to figure out a different method. I created an algorithm that could generate a page of text by taking the index number as an input, without needing to store anything.[1] The index number was indistinguishable from the ones that used to refer to the name of a file stored on disk, and the result was the same — every time a user visited a "location" in the library (the indices contain hexagon name, wall, shelf, and volume number), they saw the same page of text there. The algorithm generating the text was a pseudorandom number generator that used the index as an input or random seed, meaning that as users progressed from one page to the next in the library, what they saw appeared random, just as it did before. In effect, nothing had changed, though underlying that, almost nothing existed.

To approach the ontological question of the presence or absence of this digital archive, it helps to compare it to digital forms with which we have more experience. Many users share the initial reaction that if nothing immediately resembling these pages of text is stored on disk, they must not exist. But consider a more typical digital archive, like a library's electronic holdings. Its texts are stored in a binary form on hard drives, most likely with some compression, and only exist in a readable form once a file is opened, yet it would not occur to us to think that when we close a PDF it ceases to exist and that it comes into existence

---

1   For those interested in greater detail: imagine a function that could take any number and convert it into a form represented by the character set of the library. The number that resulted would be a base-29 representation of the input — so 1 would become a, 2 b, 3 c, 30 would be aa, and so on until you reached $29^{3,200}-1$, which would be a page of 3,200 periods. This algorithm can generate every permutation of a page of text, and stores nothing on disk, but lacks the randomness essential to Borges's library. To restore this irrationality, I created a pseudorandom number generator (PRNG) to randomize the relationship of index to text. The index number is used as the input of this algorithm, which outputs a number anywhere between 0 and $29^{3,200}$. This random-seeming output is then converted into a page of text (a base-29 number). The PRNG algorithm I used is invertible, which means that one can take a page of text and run the formula backwards to calculate its index in the library. This is how a "search" is performed.

from nothing when we open it again. The algorithm making libraryofbabel.info possible does not perform any compression, because the index number, which is an equivalent amount of data, needs to be entered in order to retrieve a page of text. They are similar though, in that both make a vast amount of data available and ultimately present in this digital and virtual sense.

Let us play the game of accident and essence with this archive. For instance, if the random number generator were removed, and it created pages of text beginning with just the letter a, followed by b, then c, and continued to pages of enormous length, with its only limit the RAM of the computer converting number into text, would this be an archive of present text? What if there were no numerical indices, but instead a user requested a page by entering a block of text and that block of text was exactly the content of the page? Is this an archive? Then what about the blank page, which holds *in potentia* any and every possible page of writing? Should we say that space, or what the Greeks called χώρα, often translated as "place," is an archive of all possible material permutations, and thus that they are all constantly present? After all, space can be shown to admit any possible contents.

We should conclude not that we can or must create rigorous criteria for being, but rather that presence and absence are deconstructible terms without absolute grounding. Virtual presences were a reminder of this instability long before they took a digital or computational form, when they were restricted, for example, to mirrors, streams, or dreams. As we consider the impossibility of totality or universality and complicate the possibility of novelty (the presence of the new), we should keep in mind that the meaning of being is also withheld.

Image and Text

When I completed the text library, I recognized that the code I created could be applied to any realm of experience, and my desire to permute grew. I began work on the Babel Image Archives (https://babelia.libraryofbabel.info), which now contain every

Fig. 6 — A randomly accessed image from babelia.libraryofbabel.info. Babelia #4973828821858677.

possible 4,096-color, 640 by 416 pixel image — about $10^{961,755}$ in total. The functioning of the image archive is almost identical. Rather than representing a number with a character set, the 4,096 colors represent the different values that can occupy each position — and the rows and columns of pixels, like the lines of text, are the sequential digits. Each image is essentially a base-4,096 number. The vast majority look like no more than colorful static (see Fig. 6).

This indistinctness is a function of entropy. Any representational image must have blocks of the same or similar colors, which would be as rare as finding a page at random in the text archive with only the letter a. Nonetheless, the image archives contain digital representations of every past and future artwork, photographs of every event that will happen in the future, and all those that won't. The extension of iterability into the visual field disrupts the classical representation of the distinction between language and experience. According to this tradition, language is a representation of reality, whereas sensory experience would provide more immediate access to things. The image archives deconstruct this distinction — a visual experience indistinguishable from the "real" one is nonetheless possible in the absence of any motivating context, including the presence of the thing it is meant to present or represent. Again, illusion, mirage, fantasy, dream, representational art, the mirror and all reflection are only possible because iterability inhabits the essence of visual experience.

Iterability generates seemingly discrete units, signs that can be repeated. The basic elements of language are letters or words — but what are the components of the visual? We shouldn't make the mistaken assumption that iterability can only affect vision in its digital form, when an image is encoded as pixels, each containing definite color information. If there are limits to what can be represented in the Babel Image Archives, it's not the case that what lies outside those limits also lies beyond the reach of iterability. We can recognize immediately that a reflection or photograph reproduces reality faithfully and often indistinguishably, and thus that the citationality of the visual does not wait for the appearance of any technology, let alone the digital, but rather makes the technical prosthesis possible. We may disagree about whether scientific or everyday experience reveals a more fundamental layer of reality, but in either case we see the essential place of iterability. Everyday experience encounters a world of objects and, following an effort of abstraction, a world of color. Both of these realms of visual experience are divided by the concept, which is itself an iterable structure. Everything we said before of the sign is true of the concept — it must be recognizable across a potentially endless number of instantiations, despite transformations of context. The experiential world of color recognizes a similarly conceptualized field, in fact a field that is more differentiated or impoverished on the basis of the refinement of the observer's knowledge of color. Nothing changes with respect to iterability when we attempt to define this field scientifically. We can define color as the impression of an amount of energy constituting something that is both wave and particle only on the basis of the accessibility of such an entity to our knowledge or experience. Because a similar result follows from similar experiments (based on the receptivity of an experimenter or mechanical sensor), we can form a concept and mathematical law to define this entity. Repeatability is essential to its status as empirically verifiable and scientifically valid.

For anything to escape iterability, it is not sufficient to point out the contingent limits of our technical reproductions or current knowledge. There will always be shortcomings to our efforts to totalize, like the constraints of the character set and size of a page on libraryofbabel.info or the number of colors and the pixel dimensions in the image archives. But a new letter, word, or color can only be added to our verbal or visual languages if it can be recognized as such, and thus if it is open to repetition. Nonetheless, we can see that neither sensory experience nor language grants access to a fundamental ground. What conforms itself to our knowledge or perception, whether as verbal or visual reality, is a representative, at least one degree removed from the imagined immediacy of things. Its iterability attests to its lack of an absolute grounding — it is equally possible in the absence of things. Yet, despite only having access to a world and a knowledge of things and concepts that is entirely unmoored, the finite depends on the infinite which transcends it. A universe of only marks would not be internally consistent, because nothing would motivate the continuous advent of arrival and change that we greet as the flux of the present moment. Our world of emissaries implies this realm of absolute things, but in order to communicate themselves to us they must conform to our sensory apparatus and conceptual structure. Thus our experience is dependent on what remains inaccessible to us.

Atomism and Eternal Return

There is a philosophical system that attempts to describe a universe of discrete elements, and one that Borges related explicitly to the idea of the universal library: the atomist tradition. According to the atomists, the great complexity of human experience is possible on the basis of the interactions of a small group of basic particles, which combine in different numbers and positions to form macroscopic structures. In "The Total Library," the essay Borges wrote two years before "The Library of Babel" to trace the history of the idea that language is possible as a combinatoric process, he finds its oldest forebears to be the atomist philosophers. Among other reasons, this should interest us because, as was argued in the first chapter, this idea is more ancient than any of its instantiations (Borges denies authorship of it, and I certainly do as well). Given that the atomists are pre-Socratic philosophers, whose writings are lost and whose ideas are recorded only in fragments and testimonia from classical writers, we could say that this idea originates *before the letter*. As an analogy to their view of the interaction of atoms accounting for sensory experience, they described language as a system where the permutations of a basic set of elements (the letters) account for the entire complexity of possible meaning. As we explored in the previous section, nothing that presents itself to our visual or verbal experience can escape the atomistic structure; nonetheless, our thesis will be that if there is anything like invention or novelty, it is dependent on the divisibility of the atom.

It's also in "The Total Library" that Borges mentions explicitly the relation between the universal library and the eternal return. He writes, "it [the Total Library] is a typographical avatar of that doctrine of the Eternal Return which, adopted by the Stoics or Blanqui, by the Pythagoreans or Nietzsche, eternally returns" (214).[2] Though we may associate the thought of eternal return with Friedrich Nietzsche, the idea has a much older history and in its most ancient formulation is based on atomistic presuppositions (though its oldest attribution, according to Borges, is to the Pythagoreans). The principles of atomistic eternal return are as follows:

1. Given a finite set of atoms, or an infinite universe (τὸ πᾶν) divided into worlds (κόσμοι) composed of finite sets of atoms,
2. an infinite time,
3. and a universe determined exclusively by mechanistic causality,

---

2   While Kane X. Faucher in "The Effect of the Atomist Clinamen in the Constitution of Borges's 'Library of Babel,'" relates the short story to the atomist tradition, he neglects the theme of eternal return that underlies all of Borges's references to atomism. Faucher identifies the letter as the atom of textuality, but claims that the clinamen of the atom would be the source of the library's permutations. This Lucretian idea accounts for the presence of chance and even freedom in the universe, and thus contradicts the mechanistic and combinatoric premises of the eternal return. His identification of an infinite, cyclical universe as "Aristotelian" (143) is also a misattribution. If one does not look too closely, one could make Aristotle resemble the atomists on this point, but the former explicitly rebuked the atomistic doctrine, because it posited the mere appearance of teleology without any intentionality. Though he is correct to question the verifiability of our narrator's universal pretensions, Faucher's conclusions that the library's texts have "a truth value of nil" and his advocacy of a "hyper-linguistic," "anagogical" reading method by which "the rise above of spirit in relation to text" overcomes the latter's "absolute lack or vacuity," demonstrates a greater ideological mystification on his own part (145).

then the atoms composing our world will necessarily exhaust their possible permutations and will begin to repeat. Because there is no intelligible causality (free will or divine intervention) which could alter the course of events, the entirety of natural and human history will repeat endlessly in the same order. We should hear echoes in this of the form of repetition we referred to as iterability and its relation to discrete units, atomic elements.

We should not make the mistake of thinking that the natural philosophy of ancient thinkers presents an outmoded way of thought and that our science has superseded or refuted these theses. The atomist philosophy developed in response to an essential problem of thought, and one that science has yet to answer definitively. It was considered in the first chapter, under the heading of Kant's antinomies of pure reason, as the necessary struggle of reason between the need for a simple substance and the impossibility of anything indivisible appearing in an infinitely divisible time and space. A simple substance, or element that cannot be further divided (an *a-tom,* that which cannot be cut), responds to an essential need of thought. The ancients looked at the basic materials of their world — for example, wood — and found a problem: no matter how much they subdivided this matter, they found at the end — smaller wood. If this process could continue endlessly, there would be no basic substance out of which wood and its properties could be built up; the stability of all macroscopic experience is drawn into question if there is no simple substance. The solution of the atomists was to simply posit (or assume) that indivisible atoms underlie all experience; these atoms' only properties were shape, position, and size, and all properties of all objects developed from the different arrangements and orientations of these simpler objects. We can already notice a problem in this theory — for atoms to have shape and size, they must be at least ideally divisible, and it would be possible, for example, to speak of the corners of a triangular atom, etc. (Waterfield 165–66). It's not at all the case that this theory was confirmed in the early twentieth century when "the atom" was first modeled by physicists. The fact that we now compose the universe not simply of atoms but of sub-atomic particles would make an Ancient Greek (or, as Borges puts it, a philologist) laugh. The essential property of the atom is not that it is microscopic but that it is indivisible — and it remains a question whether it would ever be possible for something indivisible to present itself to empirical investigation, or whether the best we can ever do is to reach a layer of reality that our technology and knowledge are no longer sufficient to divide.

To approach Borges's thoughts about the eternal return, it's helpful to go by way of Nietzsche. Certain tendencies in Borges's fleeting, playful discourse will be more intelligible when we have explored a similar technique in his predecessor. Perhaps the most important trait shared by the two authors is a capacity for self-contradiction that we have already seen at work in the interplay between Borges's fiction and non-fiction. Nietzsche, too, engages in this practice which draws into question the most fundamental assumptions of the philosophical tradition: that reason is a universally sovereign unity of thought and that rational discourse implies a rational subject with the same incapacity for self-contradiction. The difficulty becomes, across this gap of ironic distance, discerning the contours of an author who may be multiple, mutable, or nowhere at all.

Nietzsche

To understand Nietzsche's writings about the eternal return, it would be helpful if one could fit them within an architectonic in which they dovetailed with the other major concepts of his philosophy. However, such an approach would begin by betraying him. His fragmentary style seethes with internal contradictions and irreconcilable principles to such an extent that one can only form coherence of it by denying and doing violence to parts of the text. The mania for division and denial in Nietzsche criticism, to create periods of his thought that consist of single works or even portions of a text, to dismiss individual sentences or aphorisms as products of madness, or to deploy the difference between published and unpublished work is ultimately an effort to divide and conquer a corpus already in the process of dividing and doing battle with itself.[3] None of these categories can ever be secure, especially in a body of work whose basic mode is internal strife. My preference is to attempt to embrace or at least to think through as many of these conflicting fragments as possible. What Nietzsche writes of the subject is just as true of the supposed author of his fractured discourse:

---

3   By no means would I belittle the philological work that sorts out the dates of Nietzsche's scattered corpus and attempts to place in order drafts, revisions, and redactions. This is important scholarship from which Nietzsche criticism can benefit. It only goes astray if it pretends that its goal is to compile a polished body of work free of contradiction, to validate or exclude fragments on the basis of agreement or dissonance with a supposed published doctrine.

One typically dismisses a draft, an early work, a late recantation, etc., if it seems to contradict what is understood as the dominant tendencies of the body of an author's work. Of course, the construction of that dominant interpretation is not neutral and depends on the very acts of exclusion that it is supposed to justify. But it is all the more paradoxical to perform such an operation with a body of work defined by its self-contradictions.

The greatest absurdities come when madness is invoked as grounds for exclusion. There is no mark that distinguishes the discourse of the mad from the sane. Moreover, the aspects of Nietzsche's fragments thought to be indicative of madness are those most characteristic of his style, which made a sport of hubris and self-overcoming. Walter Kaufmann is right to defend much of Nietzsche's work (everything from *Thus Spake Zarathustra* to *Ecce Homo*) from critics who would dismiss it as products of madness. However, he makes two related gestures that undermine this defense: a) He argues not for the undecidability of sanity and madness, but for the sanity of Nietzsche's work on the basis of an "organic unity" inimical to his corpus (Kaufmann 70), and b) he is still willing to invoke madness to discredit a fragment that conflicts with his critical or editorial positions (455–57). His strange argumentation in this case merits being studied in full, along with all the places where he reads madness on the grounds of a lack of "inhibition" in Nietzsche. For example, Nietzsche's signing a letter "Dionysius" is attributed to madness breaking down his "inhibitions" (Kaufmann 33). This play with the signature is a sign of madness only if all literature is mad—was the one who wrote the name "Zarathustra" a decade earlier mad? What about the eighteen-year-old whose autobiography began, "As a plant, I was born close to the graveyard" (qtd. in Köhler 1)?

The body and physiology as the starting point: why? — We gain the correct idea of the nature of our subject-unity, namely as regents at the head of a communality (not as "souls" or "life forces"), also of the dependence of these regents upon the ruled and of an order of rank and division of labor as the conditions that make possible the whole and its parts [...]. The relative ignorance in which the regent is kept concerning individual activities and even disturbances within the communality is among the conditions under which rule can be exercised. In short, we also gain a valuation of *not-knowing,* of seeing things on a broad scale, of simplification and falsification, of perspectivity. (*Will to Power* 271).

Underneath a body or corpus we place the unity of a subject only at the expense of the dissimulation of these "disturbances within the communality."

The eternal return can to some extent contribute to the revaluation of all values, Nietzsche's response to nihilism. He offers a genealogical explanation of nihilism, deriving it from the Platonic and Christian traditions which placed all value and truth in a transcendent, immutable realm. Atheism denied the existence of this realm, but it took hold in Europe without questioning the first premise of Christianity — that our world was worthless. As Nietzsche explains, "A nihilist is a man who judges of the world as it is that it ought not to be, and of the world as it ought to be that it does not exist" (318). The eternal return can contribute to the overcoming of nihilism by subverting some basic Christian assumptions. Christianity foretells a final judgment at the end of this existence, which places a final seal on the value of our actions and existence by determining if we are worthy of admittance into the eternal immutability of heaven. But according to the theory of the eternal return, there is only this world endlessly, and thus finding a value in this existence cannot be deferred or cast off into a transcendent realm. Aphorism 341 of *The Gay Science,* the first explicit mention of the eternal return in Nietzsche's work, suggests that from the point of view of nihilism the repetition of this life is a great burden, but poses the question, "how well disposed would you have to become to yourself and to life to long for nothing more fervently than for this ultimate eternal confirmation and seal?" (194–95).

Other aspects of the revaluation of values place in question some of his statements about the eternal return. The highest truths, according to the classical tradition that Nietzsche sees as the seed of nihilism, are those which are true universally, independent of the time and space in which they are tested and of the observer holding them true. The logical categories are seen as highest, according to this tradition, because of their independence from the particulars of this life — they apply to everything equally, as nothing can be without substance and accident, quantity and quality, and so on. Even if they may be, according to Aristotle, dependent on the existence of substance, they are not dependent on this or that substance, but rather nothing can be without being as a substance and without each of these categories applying to it. Nietzsche inverts this transcendentalism and places the categories in the service of life:

> The inventive force that invented categories labored in the service of our needs, namely of our need for security, for quick understanding on the basis of signs and sounds, for means of abbreviation: — "substance," "subject," "object," "being," "becoming," have nothing to do with metaphysical truths. (277)

What was understood to have a value because of its independence from life is recast as having a value exclusively for the sake of life.

This revaluation complicates many of Nietzsche's later statements about the eternal return. These often sound as though they are traditionally atomist in form (though he substitutes "centers of force" for atoms):

> If the world may be thought of as a certain definite quantity of force and as a certain definite number of centers of force — and every other representation remains indefinite

and therefore useless — it follows that, in the great dice game of existence, it must pass through a calculable number of combinations. In infinite time, every possible combination would at some time or another be realized; more: it would be realized an infinite number of times. (549)

This argument relies on necessary chains of cause and effect, one of the logical categories Nietzsche has claimed is a superimposition on and falsification of the play of forces. As we try to understand what would be left over if we strip the categories from our conception of things, we must remember that we are not dispelling ideology to access an underlying truth. The measure of our interpretation can no longer be its truth, which is not a value in itself, but rather its relation to the will to power: "The criterion of truth resides in the enhancement of the feeling of power" (290). Nietzsche refers to the world without cause and effect as a mutual struggle of forces, the difference being that there is no substance underlying the changes and gathering them in a unity of identity. Without substance or cause and effect, all knowledge and all temporal progression are impossible — from one moment to the next, there is a recurrent mass of identity-less and formless forces. Nietzsche often debunks teleology with the argument that "if the world had a goal, it must have been reached" (546). This can be understood as an atomist argument: given the infinitude of time, any ultimate state it could tend toward would have been reached already. But Nietzsche always presents this diktat without anything like a logical argument or sufficient ground. It sounds to my ear, or my will to power, like an expression of the mutual struggle of forces: were it possible for becoming to reify itself as being, that would happen in the first instant, and remain so forever more. As this does not happen, we are left with an eternal return of the same in every moment, the constant advent of an undifferentiated field of forces in the new moment of becoming.

There is one last contradiction we should consider in Nietzsche's writings on the eternal return, one which deals with everything we have been discussing regarding the possibility of novelty and its relationship to the divisibility of the atom. We already heard the atomistic premises which at times he combines with his thought of eternal recurrence: "a certain definite number of centers of force." How, then, should we interpret aphorism 617 from *The Will to Power,* which brings the eternal return in explicit dialogue with the idea of will to power: "to impose upon becoming the character of being — that is the supreme will to power [...]. That *everything recurs* is the closest a*pproximation of a world of becoming to a world of being:* — high point of the meditation" (330, my emphasis), and seems to relate novelty to an explicit contradiction of his earlier atomistic premises: "Becoming as invention [...]. Instead of 'cause and effect' the mutual struggle of that which becomes, often with the absorption of one's opponent; the number of becoming elements not constant" (331). This "number of becoming elements" can only be what was earlier held to be definite in number — the centers of force. It would be possible, as I mentioned before, to claim these fragments belong to different periods of thought and represent a change in Nietzsche's thinking (they were, according to Walter Kaufmann, written about five years apart). But any such gesture relies on the untenable position that a contradiction should not occur — in this discourse rife with them, and which places in question the value of truth and the principle of contradiction. Why then express himself by means of this contradiction? Because there is a certain world-without-us, infinite or absolute quality to the struggle of forces without identity or teleology, and it is the burden and possibility of a finite consciousness to overcome it by a knowledge Nietzsche celebrates for its falsehood: "Knowledge-in-itself in a world of becoming is impossible; so how is knowledge possible? As error concerning oneself, as will to power, as will to deception" (330). The possibility of something like novelty depends on the fallibility the narrator of "The Library of Babel" complained of when viewing his tremulous, imperfect penmanship — it depends on this very difference-from-self of the mark.

Borges

Despite the complexity of Nietzsche's writing on the subject, Borges attributes unambiguously to his predecessor the atomistic form of the eternal return, criticizes this view, then posits a version that is closer to the one we unearthed in Nietzsche. It is not at all the case that Borges is a careless reader, and, given his habit of blending truth and fiction, one can never discredit the possibility that he has played a game with us, perhaps pretending to supersede Nietzsche to let his Will to Power as Will to Art forge a seeming novelty out of the eternal return of the same. Ultimately, we can find a similar expression of the impossibility of novelty at every moment in Borges, coupled with a similar contradiction focused on the divisibility or indivisibility of the atom. Again, our task will be the interpretation of a text at odds with itself.

Borges's explicit writing about Nietzsche and eternal return comes in two essays included in *Historia de la eternidad,* "The Doctrine of Cycles" and "Circular Time." The former offers an interesting demystification of the origin story Nietzsche offered for his central doctrine. In *Ecce Homo,* Nietzsche claims the inspiration for *Thus Spoke Zarathustra* (and much else besides) struck him while passing a pyramidal boulder[4] by the Lake of Silvaplana, which he jotted down on a page signed with the

---

4 The pyramid makes its appearance often enough in the course of our study to produce a sort of paranoia, or at least to merit further consideration. In addition to this *mächtigen pyramidal aufgethürmten Block,* we have already crossed paths with "O time, thy pyramids," a citation that multiplies across the pages of past and future texts. For Nietzsche it seems to be a symbol of the very eternity of the eternal return, perhaps with reference to the ancient and monumental Egyptian structures. For Shakespeare it is a symbol of the frivolity of finitude, which attempts to dress up as novel an enduring, unchanging sameness. Perhaps Shakespeare and Borges have the same monuments in mind, but emphasize their aspect as tombs, disguising a central absence? While a full contemplation of this theme would need to take into account Hegel's semiology and the *a* of differance, we will break off merely by observing that "Perhaps universal history is the history of the various intonations of a few metaphors" (Borges, "Pascal's Sphere" 353).

phrase "6,000 feet beyond men and time" (119). But Nietzsche was a classicist and couldn't possibly have been ignorant of the atomist tradition from which his idea originated or returned. Regardless, Borges in this essay attributes a rigorously atomist form of the eternal return to Nietzsche and claims to refute the latter by invoking the principle of uncountable infinity from Cantor's set theory — that is, the infinite divisibility of time and space, and thus the impossibility of the atom. Though such a criticism should eliminate the possibility of repetition, Borges ends by upping the ante of eternal return: "If Zarathustra's hypothesis is accepted, I do not understand how two identical processes keep from agglomerating into one. Is mere succession, verified by no one, enough?" (122). Such a question is much closer to Borges's typical mode of investigation than the mathematical and scientific invocations he relies on to refute Nietzsche in the rest of the essay. The idea that all experience reduces itself to a single basic form, as well as all art and all time, repeats so often throughout his work (often in identical words and passages) that he could only have chuckled to himself every time he allowed it to return. "I tend to return eternally to the Eternal Return," he acknowledges in the first words of "Circular Time," and even this witticism appeared two years earlier in "The Total Library." In the conclusion to "Circular Time," Borges considers the principle that "universal history is the history of a single man" and concludes that "the number of human perceptions, emotions, thoughts, and vicissitudes is limited, and that before dying we will exhaust them all" (228). The patriarchal language in this formulation ("*de un solo hombre*") is perhaps symptomatic of the abstraction necessary to make such a claim — it may be that gender difference, among others, prevents the formation of such a universal representative.

This immanent version of the eternal return has its textual avatar as well. In addition to his many comments about the single destiny of "man," Borges is also led by his skepticism and idealism (denying the appearance of difference and reducing it to the unity of an idea) to treat all authorship as a unitary act, writing the same book endlessly. In a poem depicting the burning of the Library of Alexandria, "Alexandria, 641 A.D." its persona, the Islamic general Omar, whom Borges tells us in a note is "a projection of the author" (*Noche* 203, my translation), affirms the eternal return: "The vigils of humanity engendered / the infinite books. If not a single one / of that plenitude remained / They would be engendered anew, each leaf and each line" (*Noche* 167, my translation). The narrator of "The Library of Babel" offered us references to both forms of eternal return as well. His final affirmation of the infinity of the library is a traditionally atomist version. He offers as premises the infinity of space (i.e., of hexagonal rooms with shelves of books) and the finite number of possible texts, and posits with his typical dogmatism: "*The Library is unlimited and Cyclical*" (*Labyrinths* 58). His conclusion is a faithful rendering of the relation of chance and necessity in atomist thought: "If an eternal traveler were to cross it in any direction, after centuries he would see that the same volumes were repeated in the same disorder (which, thus repeated, would be an order: the Order)" (58). The eternal return we identified as Nietzsche's, and which Borges's idealism approaches, also has its parallel in the cabbalistic text[5] described by the narrator: "These phrases, at first glance incoherent, can no doubt be justified in a cryptographical or allegorical manner [...]. I cannot combine some characters *dhcmrlchtdj* which the divine Library has not foreseen and which in one of its secret tongues do not contain a terrible meaning" (57). We are again in a position where we can learn from Borges's narrator, despite his ideology. If the number of possible languages bestowing a potential meaning on anything resembling a phrase is nonfinite, and if a cryptographic formula is possible by which any phrase, page, or book could be transformed into any other, and if the literal meaning (as though this distinction were secure) of that ciphered or deciphered text could be transformed metaphorically or allegorically into any possible meaning, then it appears as

---

5   The method of interpretation favored by our narrator is one Borges has elsewhere referred to as Kabbalistic; he has called any text subjected to it "a mechanism of infinite purposes" ("Kabbalah" 86).

though every text is capable of every possible meaning. Like the world of formless and identity-less forces that repeats at every moment, we have in this case the eternal return of the same text, one admitting all possible meanings and interpretations and constantly transforming into every other text with indifference.

Just as Nietzsche before him, Borges presents the experience of a finite creature as a contradiction to the premises of any eternal return. In "For Bernard Shaw," Borges considers in unison the thinking machine of Ramon Llull, which combined subject and predicates combinatorially, J.S. Mill's fear that we would run out of novel musical compositions, and Lasswitz's "chaotic library." In typical fashion, Borges suggests that each of these ideas, including the universal library that formed the subject of one of his most haunting fictions, "may make us laugh" (*Inquisitions* 163). Beyond the dismissive tone, we also find his most profound criticism of these fears of exhaustibility: "Literature is not exhaustible, for the sufficient and simple reason that a single book is not" (164). We have returned to the property of difference-from-self, which guarantees that the purported atoms of a textual eternal return will in fact be divisible. He defines a book as "the dialogue with the reader" and asserts that "That dialogue is infinite" (163). Our finite, fallible knowledge guarantees something like novelty, as impossibility of the saturation of context or meaning.

The universal library is itself the locus of this dialectic. Its every instantiation has a precursor, to the point where we located its essence in iterability, a property residing in the essence of language and existing before the letter. Nonetheless, a pure repetition without difference is never possible, as Borges reminds us when he says that two events without difference would be indistinguishable. Thus, every instantiation of the library brings something like novelty with it, precisely because it fails to realize the totality or universality of its ideal. While Borges's librarians searched for the justification of their existence and arcana for the future and found mostly lines resembling surrealist juxtapositions, the visitors to libraryofbabel.info are just as likely to search for internet memes or ASCII art. The infinite dialogue continues.

Both Nietzsche and Borges show a sly self-assurance when expressing themselves by means of contradiction, drawing power from both sides of the polemic they straddle. In Nietzsche, this tendency shows an affirmation in the face of the impossibility of totality, which can neither be reduced to the forgetting of Being nor embedded in a unitary history and project of metaphysics issued forth from Being itself.[6] Borges's elusive acknowledgement of his own openness to contradiction is spoken in the voice of an artist and philosopher; he calls it his "tendency […] to evaluate religious or philosophical ideas on the basis of their aesthetic worth and even for what is singular and marvelous about them. Perhaps this is an indication of a basic skepticism [*escepticismo esencial*]" (189). Both authors express the possibility of a transcendence of limitations that can only be partial and unconfirmed, without absolute grounding. For there to be experience at all, things must conform to the form of iterable concepts and signs, which Nietzsche refers to as a tool of survival. Nonetheless, it is the ineluctable incompleteness of our knowledge (or the essential property of the iterable sign) that makes something like novelty possible. If there is always discovery in invention, as our creations always conform to the forms of possible knowledge and expression, there is still an invention in discovery, as even our greatest efforts toward fidelity rely on the unstable and never self-identical atom. Borges and Nietzsche opt for one of the possible modes of expression of this conflict, the affirmation that hides and elides a negation.

---

6 See Derrida's "Interpreting Signatures (Nietzsche/Heidegger): Two Questions" for the preliminary indications of a deconstruction of Heidegger's *Nietzsche,* whose project to treat Will To Power and Eternal Return as the names of essence and existence in a metaphysical project betrays Nietzsche by attempting to totalize his thought.

In Which It Is Argued, Despite Popular Opinion to the Contrary, That Borges Did Not Invent the Internet

Our theme has not been the digital realization of an author's fantasy but the deferral of presence across several virtualities. So I'll conclude with a consideration of a trend in the recent criticism of Borges that I find in its most extreme forms highly suspect: the effort to cast him as a prophet of the internet and related digital technologies. Though these critics may intend to pay homage to a visionary author, there is just as much in their work that suggests an ideology of technological progress, which obscures essential aspects of both Borges's text and contemporary culture.

These authors have diverse ways of framing and justifying their studies. Borges "anticipates hypertext and the internet" (Sassón-Henry, "Borges and Moulthrop" 11), he is a "forerunner of the technology of the new millenium" (Sassón-Henry, *Futures* iii), his stories are "metaphors for cyberspace and the internet" (Acuña-Zumbado 642, my translation), and "embody some characteristics of hypertext and the World Wide Web" (Sassón, *Borges 2.0* 11). While the language of anticipation, the forerunner, and the proto-trace speaks to a perceived anachronism in Borges's work, the language of embodiment and metaphor suggests his role as artist — not to create literal technology but merely to prefigure and herald it. How is it that Borges performs this literary act of foreshadowing? These writers do their best to identify the relevant traits in his work, claiming to see a break with linear temporality, the creation of multiple levels of meaning (at one point, Sassón-Henry counts three), intertextuality, and the necessity of the active participation of the reader. At this point, the careful reader might be justified to protest that these are qualities of every text as text, regardless of its status as hyper- or proto-hyper-. It suffices to recall what the narrator-librarian taught us about the nonfinite possibilities of cryptographical and allegorical meaning, and the multifaceted, non-linear text necessarily resulting from them, to remind ourselves that no act of reading can ever be passive. We then need to question the status of prophet or literary prefiguration, by asking what if anything hypertext has introduced that would represent a rupture? For some time now we have been considering the unverifiability of novelty, which is only possible as impossible. There are certainly differences in our encounter with what goes by the name of hypertext, but these differences are abyssal, without any concept to secure their certainty, and never constitute something recognizable as an essence. The words of any printed text can be placed online and made accessible with a hyperlink. Does the work thereby become hypertextual? Was it already? If we can introduce in a textual body the referentiality of a hyperlink, allowing one text to burrow into another, it is only because this intertextuality was implicit in every text as such. Since no rigorous criterion separates hypertext from plaintext (and never mind distinguishing proto-hyper-text), we can no more claim that Borges is our predecessor or prophet than we can claim to have advanced beyond his textual moment. We are all contemporaries in being anachronistic with ourselves.[1]

---

1   J. Andrew Brown, in "Retasking Borges: Technology and the Desire for a Borgesian Present," his review of several of the works we will consider in this chapter, offers a more generous reading. He draws from Borges's "Kafka and his Precursors" to invert the order of causality, to suggest that we, immersed in hypertext, create its predecessors by the act of looking for them.

Beyond the experience or form of the text, these same critics point to the content of certain stories ("The Library of Babel" and "The Garden of Forking Paths," typically) as similarly prescient. These interpretations are marked by both their excesses and their deficiencies: "In 'The Library of Babel,' Borges's [*sic*] portrays man's inability to find the infinite and perfect book. Thus, Borges seems to prophesy the predicament of those in the twenty-first century who attempt to find the answers to their problems in the internet" (Sassón-Henry, *Borges 2.0* 53). It is correct to recognize the absence of absolute knowledge as a continuity between internet users and book readers of all times, though our dual question remains — what has changed for us that merits the search for its precursors, and what is different about Borges that merits his election as such?

Martin S. Watson exhibits this same mystification — a misreading of Borges and a misreading of the contemporary moment. The infinity of the library is repeatedly asserted in his text ("the infinite archive" [151]), and the same mistake is made with respect to Ramón Llull's thinking machine. Of this simple and limited permutation, it is claimed, "The machine contains infinity because of the endless possibilities for combination and recombination" (154). This is more than just bad math. We must recognize, with some dismay, that if "The Library of Babel" has been misread in accordance with the ideology of its narrator, it is thought of as an appropriate comparison because of an identical misinterpretation about what Watson calls "today's digital world" (154). He imagines that we have infinite knowledge: "'The Library of Babel' is an apt metaphor for the posthuman experience of the archive because it captures the enormous realms of information that are currently available" (159). This comparison demonstrates as much a misapprehension of the past, seeing Borges's work as different from its time in resembling ours, as a misapprehension of the present, seeing us as novel enough to merit comparison with the Borges who never was.

Placing in question the novelty or even the auto-contemporaneity of our "own" present further destabilizes the order of causality.

The conceptual framework Sassón-Henry uses to set Borges apart from other writers demonstrates that the belief in the essential novelty of our technology is in truth an affirmation of the ideals of humanism. This is most apparent in the logocentrism underlying her comparison of our "postprint" present to a "preprint" past taking place before the letter. She celebrates oral literacy for the immediate presence of speaker and recipient, then claims that hypertext restores what print loses by allowing users to comment on writing and by reconstituting the processes of thought ("hypertext imitates the mental process of association" [*Borges 2.0* 15]). It shouldn't be necessary to point out that these distinctions deconstruct themselves, as speaker and recipient never have immediate presence to each other or even presence-to-self, but we can at least witness the bad faith of the gesture by which Borges escapes his fate as a print author: "Borges, who through his superb use of language manages to exceed the limits of print" (Sassón-Henry, *Borges 2.0* 16). How certain, then, can we be that these were limits, or that they were limits of print alone? This claim depends on the aforementioned idea that the reader takes an active part only in stories written by Borges (Cortázar is one of the only other authors allowed a comparison in her study). She concludes with a strange invocation of literary theory:

> By undermining the role of the author, Borges presents to the literary world two ideas that supplement each other: (1) the author vanishes from the literary act and (2) the reader moves into the text through the space left open by the author. These tenets relate to the ideas expressed by Roland Barthes in his essay "The Death of the Author." (*Borges 2.0* 19)

While we should question why this vanishing of the author is now a virtue just a few pages after her paean to orality, we also need to point out that the death of the author is not a contingent feature of this or that text, whether pre-, post-, or hyper-, but of everything expressed in language and subject to iterability. Attributing it to the sovereign decision of a writer's "superb use of language" attempts to shore up dissemination within the subject present to itself, another celebration of logocentrism.[2]

Our study has attempted to show the continuity of something like an essence underlying the various forms of the universal library, as a philosopher's thought experiment, a fictional narrative, or a technological "invention." We may be tempted to invoke the τέχνη of the Greeks in classifying this shared nature of art and technology, though what these have in common is not the security of an identical essence but the rupture of a ceaseless differing-from-self. The iterability that allows language to be wrested from the context of a speaker's intention and appear as a purely combinatoric, mechanical process is also what prevents this project from ever completing itself by saturating the

---

2   In a work that predates these by a generation, *Borges y la Intelegencia Artificial,* Ema Lapidot considers the relationship of Borges's writing to thinking machines. Her study shares several common *topoi* with the more recent work on the subject; for example, Borges's stories are described as "metaphors for the essential components of modern thinking machines" (61, my translation), the creative role of the reader is foregrounded, and the permutations of Llull's thinking machine are counted as infinite. However, she reads Borges as refuting any comparison between human faculties and those of machines.

Lapidot sees "The Library of Babel" as demonstrating a mechanistic creative process that is unable to imitate the poetic, emotive inspiration of human beings. She claims that Borges, "does not take seriously the mechanization of literature" (26, my translation), and identifies his work with an inimical humanism: "We can accept without difficulty the mechanization of logical thoughts, but we detest the idea of mechanizing what is specifically human: our special mode of perceiving the universe and our extraordinary ability to express it" (153, my translation).

Lapidot thus avoids the error of exaggerating the prowess of technology (as well as the twin error of reading that absolutization back into Borges). However, she makes the opposite mistake of absolutizing human intelligence to rescue it from technicity. "The Library of Babel" shows us that both our most logical and our most poetic or mystical creations are reproducible and iterable in this machinic fashion. If we would like to believe in our own creativity or freedom, the challenge is to think it together with the machine. It would not be possible to reconcile her position with a line she quotes from an intriguing interview Borges gave on the subject in 1967, where he says of poetry: "There's always a little of 'The Library of Babel' there! There's a little of the machine…" (qtd. in Lapidot 24, my translation).

field of possible expression or meaning. We find our suspicion confirmed on every page that these authors imagine our digital technologies to have totalized the possibilities of expression and communication, and they misread Borges as envisioning the possibility of that totalization. Instead, he succeeds in predicting our contemporary moment because he expresses the lack of totality, the finitude and uncertainty that plague even the grandest projects of any cognition shuttling between uniqueness and iterability. We can also glimpse, behind the shroud of ironic distance, the corner of the smile that recognizes in this finitude the possibility of all play.

Works Cited

Acuña-Zumbado, Eduardo. "Trazos Proto-hipertextuales En La Narrative Moderna Latinoamericana: 'La Biblioteca De Babel.'" *Hispania* 95.4 (2012): 640–49. JSTOR. Web. 20 Nov. 2015.

Alazraki, Jaime. *Borges and the Kabbalah.* Cambridge: Cambridge UP, 1988. Print.

Apostol, Gina. "Borges, Politics, and the Postcolonial." *Los Angeles Review of Books* (2013). 18 Aug. 2013. Web. 24 Nov. 2015. <https://lareviewofbooks.org/essay/borges-politics-and-the-postcolonial>.

Badmington, Neil. "Babelation." *Cy-Borges: Memories of the Posthuman in the Work of Jorge Luis Borges.* Eds. Stefan Herbrechter and Ivan Callus. Lewisburg: Bucknell UP, 2009. 59–70. Print.

Balderston, Daniel. *Out of Context: Historical Reference and the Representation of Reality in Borges.* Durham: Duke UP, 1993. Print.

Barrenechea, Ana María. *Borges: The Labyrinth Maker.* Trans. Robert Lima. New York: New York UP, 1965. Print.

Basile, Jonathan. "Theory — Why Hexagons 1." *libraryofbabel. info.* Jonathan Basile, Mar. 2015. Web. 18 Nov. 2015. <https://libraryofbabel.info/theory.html>.

The Bible. *New Revised Standard Version.* 1989. Bible Gateway. Web. 25 Nov. 2015.

Bloch, William Goldbloom. *The Unimaginable Mathematics of Borges' Library of Babel.* Oxford: Oxford UP, 2008. Print.

Borges, Jorge Luis. "The Argentine Writer and Tradition." 1951. Trans. Esther Allen. *The Total Library: Non-fiction 1922–1986*. Ed. Eliot Weinberger. London: Penguin, 1999. 225–28. Print.

———. "An Autobiographical Essay." *The Aleph and Other Stories 1933–1969: Together with Commentaries and an Autobiographical Essay*. Trans. Norman Thomas di Giovanni. London: J. Cape, 1971. 135–85. Print.

———. "La Biblioteca De Babel." *Obras Completas*. Buenos Aires: Emecé, 1974. 465–71. Print.

———. "La Biblioteca Total." *Ficcionario: Una Antología De Sus Textos*. Ed. Emir Rodríguez Monegal. México, D.F.: Fondo De Cultura Económica, 1985. 126–29. Print.

———. *The Book of Sand: The Gold of the Tigers, Selected Lated Poems*. Trans. Norman Thomas di Giovanni. Harmondsworth: Penguin, 1979. PDF.

———. *Borges at 80: Conversations*. Ed. Willis Barnstone. Bloomington: Indiana UP, 1982. Epub.

———. "Circular Time." 1941. Trans. Esther Allen. *The Total Library: Non-fiction 1922–1986*. Ed. Eliot Weinberger. London: Penguin, 1999. 225–28. Print.

———. "A Defense of Basilides the False." 1932. Trans. Eliot Weinberger. *The Total Library: Non-fiction 1922–1986*. Ed. Eliot Weinberger. London: Penguin, 1999. 65–68. Print.

———. "A Defense of the Kabbalah." 1932. Trans. Eliot Weinberger. *The Total Library: Non-fiction 1922–1986*. Ed. Eliot Weinberger. London: Penguin, 1999. 83–86. Print.

———. "The Doctrine of Cycles." 1936. Trans. Esther Allen. *The Total Library: Non-fiction 1922–1986*. Ed. Eliot Weinberger. London: Penguin, 1999. 115–22. Print.

———. *The Garden of Branching Paths*. Trans. Norman Thomas di Giovanni. libraryofbabel.info. Web. 2 Dec. 2015. <https://libraryofbabel.info/Borges/thegardenofbranchingpaths.pdf>.

———. "Historia De La Noche." *Obras Completas*. Vol. II. Barcelona: Emecé, 1989. 165–203. Print.

———. "A History of Angels." 1926. Trans. Esther Allen. *The Total Library: Non-fiction 1922–1986.* Ed. Eliot Weinberger. London: Penguin, 1999. 16–19. Print.

———. "A History of the Echoes of a Name." 1955. Trans. Eliot Weinberger. *The Total Library: Non-fiction 1922–1986.* Ed. Eliot Weinberger. London: Penguin, 1999. 405–08. Print.

———. *El jardín de senderos que se bifurcan.* Buenos Aires: Sur, 1942. Print.

———. "John Wilkins' Analytical Language." 1942. Trans. Eliot Weinberger. *The Total Library: Non-fiction 1922–1986.* Ed. Eliot Weinberger. London: Penguin, 1999. 229–32. Print.

———. "The Library of Babel." *Ficciones.* Trans. Anthony Kerrigan. New York: Grove, 1962. 79–88. Print.

———. "The Library of Babel." *Collected Fictions.* Trans. Andrew Hurley. New York: Viking, 1998. Print.

———. "The Library of Babel." Trans. James East Irby. *Labyrinths: Selected Stories & Other Writings.* New York: New Directions Pub., 1964. 51–58. Print.

———. "On the Cult of Books." 1951. Trans. Eliot Weinberger. *The Total Library: Non-fiction 1922–1986.* Ed. Eliot Weinberger. London: Penguin, 1999. 358–62. Print.

———. *Other Inquisitions: 1937–1952.* Trans. Ruth L.C. Simms. New York: Simon and Schuster, 1965. Print.

———. "Pascal's Sphere." 1951. Trans. Eliot Weinberger. *The Total Library: Non-fiction 1922–1986.* Ed. Eliot Weinberger. London: Penguin, 1999. 351–53. Print.

———. "The Total Library." 1939. Trans. Eliot Weinberger. *The Total Library: Non-fiction 1922–1986.* Ed. Eliot Weinberger. London: Penguin, 1999. 214–16. Print.

Borges, Jorge Luis, and Norman Thomas di Giovanni. *Autobiografía 1899–1970.* Buenos Aires: El Ateneo, 1999. Print.

Brown, J. Andrew. "Retasking Borges: Technology and the Desire for a Borgesian Present." *Variaciones Borges* 28 (2009): 231–40. Print.

De Man, Paul. *Allegories of Reading: Figural Language in Rousseau, Nietzsche, Rilke, and Proust.* New Haven: Yale UP, 1979.

———. "A Modern Master." *Critical Essays on Jorge Luis Borges.* Ed. Jaime Alazraki. Boston: G.K. Hall, 1987. 55–62. Print

Derrida, Jacques. "Des Tours De Babel." Trans. Joseph F. Graham. *Acts of Religion.* Ed. Gil Anidjar. New York: Routledge, 2002. 102–34. Print.

———. "Interpreting Signatures (Nietzsche/Heidegger): Two Questions." *Philosophy and Literature* 10.2 (1986): 246–62. Print.

———. "Signature Event Context." *Limited Inc.* Baltimore: Johns Hopkins UP, 1977. Print.

di Giovanni, Norman Thomas. "The Borges Papers." Lucerna. Web. 18 Nov. 2015. <http://www.digiovanni.co.uk/borges. htm>.

Faucher, Kane X. "The Effect of the Atomist Clinamen in the Constitution of Borges's 'Library of Babel.'" *Variaciones Borges* 23 (2007): 129–47. Print.

———. "A Few Ruminations on Borges' Notions of Library and Metaphor." *Variaciones Borges* 12 (2001): 125–37. Print.

Fernandez, Antonio Toca. "La biblioteca de babel: Una modesta propuesta." *Revista Casa Del Tiempo* III.24 (2009): 77–80. Difusión Cultural. Universidad Autónoma Metropolitana. Web. 18 Nov. 2015. <http://www.uam.mx/difusion/ casadeltiempo/24_iv_oct_2009/casa_del_tiempo_eIV_ num24_77_80.pdf>.

Foucault, Michel. "Language to Infinity." *Language, Countermemory, Practice: Selected Essays and Interviews.* Trans. Donald F. Bouchard and Sherry Simon. Ithaca: Cornell UP, 1977. 53–67. Print.

Grau, Cristina. *Borges y la Arquitectura.* Madrid: Cátedra, 1989. Print.

James, Clive. "Borges' Bad Politics." *Clive's Lives: A Guide to Twentieth Century Culture. Slate,* 7 Feb. 2007. Web. 24 Nov. 2015. <http://www.slate.com/articles/news_and_politics/ clives_lives/2007/02/jorge_luis_borges.html>.

Jarkowski, Anibal. "Cuando Borges Perdió Por Mayoría De Votos." *Clarín.* 02 Jan. 2012. Web. 04 Jan. 2017. <http://www.

clarin.com/literatura/borges-el-jardin-de-los-senderos-que-se-bifurcan-ficciones_0_HyKoJY3Dmg.html>.

Kaufmann, Walter. *Nietzsche: Philosopher, Psychologist, Antichrist.* Princeton: Princeton UP, 1950. Print.

Köhler, Joachim. *Zarathustra's Secret: The Interior Life of Friedrich Nietzsche.* Trans. Ronald Taylor. New Haven: Yale UP, 2002. Print.

Kristal, Efraín. *Invisible Work: Borges and Translation.* Nashville: Vanderbilt UP, 2002. Print.

———. "UCLA Professor Erain [*sic*] Kristal Delivers the 118th Faculty Research Lecture on 'Jorge Luis Borges.'" UCLA 118th Faculty Research Lecture. UCLA, Los Angeles. 13 May 2015. YouTube. Web. 4 Jan. 2017. <https://www.youtube.com/watch?v=oXR9AiqRXVQ>.

Lapidot, Ema. *Borges y La Inteligencia Artificial: Análisis Al Estilo De Pierre Menard.* Madrid: Ed. Pliegos, 1990. Print.

Lasswitz, Kurd. "The Universal Library." Trans. Willy Ley. *Fantasia Mathematica: Being a Set of Stories, Together with a Group of Oddments and Diversions, All Drawn from the Universe of Mathematics.* Ed. Clifton Fadiman. New York: Simon and Schuster, 1958. 237–43. Print.

Ley, Willy. "Postscript to 'The Universal Library.'" *Fantasia Mathematica: Being a Set of Stories, Together with a Group of Oddments and Diversions, All Drawn from the Universe of Mathematics.* Ed. Clifton Fadiman. New York: Simon and Schuster, 1958. 244–47. Print.

Nietzsche, Friedrich Wilhelm. *The Gay Science: With a Prelude in German Rhymes and an Appendix of Songs.* Ed. Bernard Williams. Trans. Josefine Nauckhoff and Adrian Del Caro. Cambridge: Cambridge UP, 2001. Print.

———. *The Will to Power.* Ed. Walter Arnold Kaufmann. Trans. R. J. Hollingdale. New York: Random House, 1967. Print.

Shakespeare, William. "Sonnet 123." *The Riverside Shakespeare: Second Edition.* Eds. G. Blakemore Evans and J.J.M. Tobin. Boston: Houghton Mifflin, 1997. 1865. Print.

Sassón, Perla. *Borges's Futures: Hypertexts, Labyrinths and Rhizomes: A Twenty-First Century Reading of "the Garden of Forking Paths" and "the Library of Babel."* Diss. U of Albany, 2000. Ann Arbor: UMI, 2001. Print.

Sassón-Henry, Perla. *Borges 2.0: From Text to Virtual Worlds.* New York: Peter Lang, 2007. Print.

———. "Borges' 'The Library of Babel' and Moulthrop's Cybertext 'Reagan Library' Revisited." *Rocky Mountain Modern Language Association* 60.2 (2006): 11–22. JSTOR. Web. 20 Nov. 2015.

Sefer Yetzirah: The Book of Creation. Trans. and ed. Aryeh Kaplan. San Francisco: Weiser Books, 1997. Print.

Sturrock, John. *Paper Tigers: The Ideal Fictions of Jorge Luis Borges.* Oxford: Clarendon, 1977. Print.

Waldman, Katy. "Jorge Luis Borges' 'Library of Babel' Is Now a Real Website. Borges Would Be Alarmed." *Slate.* 30 Apr. 2015. Web. 25 Oct. 2015. <http://www.slate.com/blogs/browbeat/2015/04/30/jonathan_basile_brings_borges_library_of_babel_to_life_with_an_eerie_gibberish.html>.

Waterfield, Robin. "The Atomists." *The First Philosophers: The Presocratics and the Sophists.* Oxford: Oxford UP, 2000.

Watson, Martin S. "Archival Imaginings." *Cy-Borges: Memories of the Posthuman in the Work of Jorge Luis Borges.* By Stefan Herbrechter and Ivan Callus. Lewisburg: Bucknell UP, 2009. 148–63. Print.

WillH. "The Structure of the Library." *libraryofbabel.info.* Jonathan Basile, 13 Oct. 2015. Web. 18 Nov. 2015. <https://libraryofbabel.info/forum/?topic=the-structure-of-the-library>.

Wolff, Theodor. *Der Wettlauf mit der Schildkröte; Gelöste und ungelöste Probleme.* Berlin: A. Scherl, 1929. Print.

"W. dreams, like Phaedrus, of an army of thinker-friends, thinker-lovers. He dreams of a thought-army, a thought-pack, which would storm the philosophical Houses of Parliament. He dreams of Tartars from the philosophical steppes, of thought-barbarians, thought-outsiders. What distance would shine in their eyes!"

— Lars Iyer

Made in the USA
Las Vegas, NV
10 November 2022